Managing Life's Tough Challenges

Finding Hope in the Storms

With Study Questions

Dr. W. Roy Sommerville

DEDICATION

To Belinda and our four children
Andrew, Jonathan, Angela & Jocelyn

I am truly blessed.

CONTENTS

Acknowledgements

Acknowledgements

I am grateful to the Queensway Baptist Church Family, Toronto, for their love for the Lord and appetite for the Word of God. Their faithful attentiveness, receptivity and responsiveness to many hundreds of my sermons over the past 12 years has been a great encouragement to me. Some of those sermons provided the raw material from which most of the chapters for this book has been quarried. So I thank them for granting me the privilege to spend time studying the Scriptures and preparing sermons, Bible Studies and lesson plans --- in short, doing that which I love. I am also indebted to those who helped get this project from idea to reality. Many thanks. Any errors found in these pages are entirely mine, and that of no one else.

Finally, a word about writing style. I have written these words in a conversational format. I write the way I preach. Hopefully, this translates into easy-to-read material. I trust that this book will be as great a blessing to those who will read it, as it has been for me to write it.

CHAPTER 1

HOPELESSNESS:

IS THIS AS GOOD AS IT GETS?

The *Titanic* was the pride of the White Star Line. She was the grandest boat ever built: in size, strength, elegance and speed. Built in Belfast, they boasted that even God couldn't sink her. But sink she did. A Titanic iceberg ripped off six boilerplate sections from the hull below the waterline. In a few hours, on April 12, 1912, on one of the calmest seas her crew had ever seen on the North Atlantic, Titanic slipped beneath the frigid surface along with 1,500 souls.

Chances are you've never been on a sinking ship. But perhaps you've experienced conditions that resemble the conditions on board a battered vessel: futility and fear, helplessness and despair --- conditions created by relational meltdown, financial crisis, spiritual drought, work challenges, an unrelenting sin struggle, or loneliness. Perhaps you've not experienced a full-bore impact that has ripped the boilerplate of the sub-surface hull of your life, but perhaps there are indications that all is not well. There's more drag than there used to be. You seem to be carrying a heavier load than yesterday. You're not making as much progress as you used to. There's a slight list. Truth be told, in some areas there's been regression. Your spiritual life, or marriage, or work, or mind, or finances used to be full of hope, health, growth, energy, and motivation. But recently, the engines of your life have slowed or stopped, and that area of your life lies dormant. Someone said, "Most men live lives of quiet desperation." Perhaps that's the only warning signal ---a sense of quiet despair. Perhaps you've wondered, "Is this as good as it gets?" Maybe you, or people you know, are facing one of life's toughest challenges and you or they are losing hope. If so, then you've picked up the right book.

The conditions in a sinking boat

There's a marine story tucked away in the Gospel of Mark in the Bible. Jesus had sent the disciples across the Sea of Galilee, while he went up into the mountain to pray. Mid-way across the lake a ferocious storm blew in, courtesy of the surrounding mountains. Peter and the rest of the disciples rowed all night into its teeth. The text said they were "troubled and tormented... for the wind was against them" (Mark 6:48 Ampl.). The climate on board the boat that night had all the conditions of a sinking ship. They would have felt trapped, for they were in the middle of the lake with nowhere to turn. They were tired, for they had been rowing all night against a strong wind. They were in over their heads literally, overwhelmed by the waves crashing overhead. They were making little or no progress, and would have been near the end of their rope, wrestling with futility and despair after moving into the fourth watch --- the darkest part of the night. They may well have felt abandoned. Jesus had ordered them into the boat and sent them across the lake. Where was He now? They were confused and afraid. The text records that they saw Jesus walking on the water, thought He was a ghost and consequently were terrified. They may also have been riddled with regret. Earlier in the day they had failed a strategic test when Jesus asked them to feed 5,000 people, and they promptly dismissed any possibility of being able to do such a thing. Then they got a close-up picture of their miscalculation and massive under-estimation of Jesus' capabilities when each of the 12 lifted a basketful of leftovers. How humbling that must have been !

Maybe you have experienced some of that in your boat – trapped, tired, overwhelmed, in despair, with regret, abandoned, confused and afraid --- and you've tried for a long time to manage those "sinking- boat-like conditions." If so, then be encouraged, for that's the theme of this book. Each chapter deals with specific tough challenges we face and must manage. You will encounter everyday issues like marriage, money and pain, and themes like stubborn destructive habit patterns, fear, guilt, temptation, relational conflicts, and many other common challenges. Before we move on though, notice the opportunity that lies in unfavourable conditions.

The opportunity in a sinking ship

The same story in Matthew 14:25-33 relates the Apostle Peter's amazing water-skiing adventure without skis, and without a ski-boat. Peter saw Jesus walking on water some distance away from the boat, and he exclaimed, "Lord... tell me to come" (v.28). Peter walked on water that night. That was an experience I'm sure Peter told over and over again to anyone willing to listen. That's what you call a "WOW" moment. That's what "wow" means: walking on water. But he wouldn't have walked on water if it hadn't been for the storm. Amazing opportunities lie in the heart of a storm. Walking-on-water opportunities are the treasure that awaits those who will view the storm through Heaven's eyes. Your challenges have the ability to make you a candidate for a walking-on-water experience with God.

Opportunity in the afterglow of crisis is a principle that runs all through Scripture. Almost every miracle in the Bible was preceded by a problem. Jesus turned water to wine, because they had run out of wine. He fed 5,000 with five loaves and two fish because the crowd was hungry and there were no Rabba stores for miles. He raised Lazarus to life, because Lazarus had already died. And Peter walked on water in the middle of a storm. The conditions in a sinking boat make you a candidate for a marvellous opportunity for God to do a miraculous work in your life. I have heard many testimonies over the years of how people came into a relationship with Christ, and it never ceases to amaze me how often Jesus Christ gets people's attention with the conditions of a sinking boat. Adverse and unfavourable conditions in your life make you a candidate for a miracle.

Then we need to seize the opportunity by stepping out of the boat onto the water. Notice that Jesus didn't come to Peter. After all, that would seem reasonable. Jesus was already on the water. Why not simply walk another few feet, and spare Peter the trouble? But no. Peter had to go to Jesus. Jesus came all the way from shore, to within a few feet of the boat, and yet Peter had to walk those final feet toward the Master. That seems to be the way it is with God. He came all the way from heaven to earth and stopped at the stoop of our hearts and waits for our invitation to come in. Every miracle requires a step of faith. Jesus draws heaven's power into a few water jugs and turns the water into wine, but He first waits for the servants to fill the jugs with water. He feeds 5,000 with five loaves and two fish, but first requires the surrender of a little boy's lunch. The walls of Jericho fell, but only after the children of Israel had walked around the city for seven days. The Red Sea split only after Moses held out his staff. The man with the withered hand got his healing only after he stretched out his deformed hand in full view of an audience. God does His part, and waits for us to do our part. That's always the way it is with God. Max Lucado puts it something like this: If there were 1,000 steps between us and heaven, God has taken 999 and left us to take just one. But it is one step that we must take. Jesus walked across the lake and invited Peter to take just a step out of the boat. But that crucial step made all the difference.

If you want to seize the opportunity in the storm and walk on water, and experience a WOW moment, you have to step out of the boat. In each of the following chapters, you will discover that God is calling you to step out of the boat. Sometimes it will be a rather small step. Other times it will be a heart-stopping, walking-on-water step. But be careful. That step will not be without its accompanying step-stopping roadblocks.

The resistance in a sinking boat

Peter must have longed to break free from the climate in the boat that night. But there were a number of factors in the boat that threatened to hold Peter back. And these same factors will threaten to hold you back.

First, Peter had to go it alone. No one else was willing to step out of the boat with him. It takes a lot of courage to go it alone. And as you face your tough challenges, you may have to go it alone

Second, Peter had to stare down the fear of the unknown. No one had ever walked on water before. This was uncharted territory. The uncertainty of what would happen the moment he stepped off the familiarity and relative safety of the known must have been formidable. It must have been frightening to look out over the side of that boat into the darkness and spray and waves, and wonder what was going to happen. Uncertainty is always present when moving in a new direction. You may have to sail uncharted waters in your journey too. The uncertainty is perhaps most frightening of all. Uncertainty conjures up questions like, "What if I fail?", "What if it gets worse?", "What will happen to me?" As you seek to step out of the boat, the road ahead will be filled with uncertainty.

The third dynamic that might have pinned Peter to the boat was the faint hope that things might get better on their own. Many passengers on the Titanic refused to believe the ship was sinking. Several things would have convinced Peter that this wasn't going to get any better on its own. He was a fisherman, and he knew the sea. This was a serious storm, they'd been in it too long, and they were tired. You need to face your situation squarely and assess its seriousness. Sometimes we won't step out of the boat until we have reached the pain threshold. In other words, we move when it hurts badly enough. Kevin Miller, in his book *Hunger for Healing,* noted that he wouldn't seek help, "until the acid of my pain ate through the walls of my denial". Sometimes we stay in the boat and miss the opportunity to break free because we deny the seriousness of the problem. Some people never miss an opportunity to miss an opportunity.

A fourth roadblock that could have anchored Peter to the boat was the pain of regret and bad memories. Earlier that day, the disciples had a faith crisis, and they doubted that Jesus could do anything to feed 5,000 men, plus women and children. Then He did the miracle with five loaves and two fish. They must have felt like such failures. Failure and the burden of regret can give us lead feet and cement overcoats.

Another thing that will threaten to hold you back is the loss of hope --- the belief that things will never improve. You get to the place where you have rowed all night, and nothing helps. There's no progress, and you begin to believe that this is as good as it gets.

For all these reasons Peter might well have missed his opportunity to walk on water, but he didn't. He overcame each of those resistance points. And it will be important in the next few pages for you to recognize the potential resistance and determine to break through them. Peter had one thing going for him that night which I believe was the key to his ability to walk on water. We might call it confidence. The Bible uses another word -- faith.

The necessity of confidence in a sinking boat

Jesus called Peter to come. The voice and presence of Jesus made all the difference. There are a number of observations in the story that can profoundly bolster your confidence. You can be confident of Christ's providence. It was Jesus who sent them out onto the lake in the first place. If you are a follower of Jesus Christ you can be certain that nothing comes into your life that has not first been Father-filtered. Second, the story indicates that Jesus went up the hill to pray. You can be certain that He was praying for the disciples in the boat. Someone once said, "There's nothing I couldn't go through if I knew Jesus Christ was in the next room praying for me." When you are going through a tough time, you can be confident that Jesus Christ is praying for you. Third, when Jesus showed up, Peter's confidence soared. You can be confident that in the midst of your storm, you have the presence of Jesus Christ. Fourth, Peter walked on water only because of the power of Christ. Notice the waves were over the disciples' heads, yet they were under Jesus' feet, and the circumstances that are over your head are also under Jesus' feet. You can be confident in His power. Finally, you can be confident of Christ's forgiveness when you fail. The story tells us that when Peter took his eyes off the Lord, he began to sink, and uttered the shortest prayer in the Bible, "Lord, save me." And Jesus did. He picked him up, and graciously walked him back to the boat.

Before you get too hard on Peter, remember that he was the only one brave enough to get out of the boat in the first place. And as you seek to break free from your sinking boat, recognize that you will probably fall and fail along the way. You may fear other people ridiculing your failure. Be prepared for that, and remember that you were willing to take the courageous step to step out and do something that many others would be afraid to do. So be confident in His grace and His willingness to forgive when you blunder.

Remember, Peter was not a man of gigantic faith. He took his eyes off Jesus and sank, and Jesus said, "Oh, you of little faith." And yet, that little faith was enough to let him walk on water. Jesus said, "faith the size of a mustard seed can move mountains" (Matthew 17:20). It's not the size of your faith that matters, it's the size of your God, the object of your faith, that's the issue. Have confidence in Him, not in the size of your faith.

If you are to manage life's tough challenges, friend, you will have to step out of the boat. You will have to take action. It won't be enough to read a book. You'll be challenged to move. What you will read in these next pages will need to enter your mind and filter down to your feet.

The purpose of a sinking boat

When Jesus and Peter boarded the boat the disciples worshipped Jesus. When God's power is evident in the midst of a storm, true worship, and renewed focus on the person of Jesus Christ, is God's intended outcome. Peter had to get out of the side of the boat and move towards Jesus. He didn't have the option of getting out the other side of the boat and walking in the opposite direction away from Jesus. Jesus said, "Come…" not "Go". Peter said "Tell me to come to you." He didn't say, "Show me how to walk on water." Walking on water was the by-product of an intentional movement toward, and focus on, the Lord Jesus Christ. Each chapter of this book will direct you to walk in a singular direction --- towards the Lord Jesus Christ. Each chapter will provide you with specific action plans. You may say, "I don't want to walk on water, I just want peace." Ah! But He wants you to walk on water. And when you've done it once, you'll want to do it again.

Putting it all together

So how do you manage life's tough challenges? First, you must establish that things must change and that change is possible. The status quo is unacceptable. The situation has deteriorated to an intolerable condition. You must establish hope that managing, surviving and overcoming your tough challenge is possible, and that there is a brighter tomorrow. Peter's first question was indicative of the kindling of hope. He shouted, "Lord, if it is you…". A person can live for 40 days without food, three days without water, eight minutes without air, but not one second without hope. The fact that you have picked up this book is an indication that at least a residue of hope is available to you. That is a great start.

Second, you need a vision of where you want to go. Peter said, "Lord, tell me to come to you." He wasn't simply interested in breaking free from the restraints of a sinking boat. He had a far greater vision than that. He wanted to come to a Person. Throughout this book I want to help you see that God wants to do so much more in your life than simply break free from the confines of whatever it is that's holding you down. He wants to offer you a personal, vibrant, life-transformational relationship with Jesus Christ. And inherent in that relationship are the adventure, significance, contentment, purpose and passion all of us long for. Bluntly put, a relationship with Jesus Christ satisfies the deepest longings of every human being on the planet.

Third, you need a plan. Peter's plan was admittedly quite simple. All he had to do was step out of the boat and cross a few yards of tumultuous tide. Simple, but not easy. Your plan may be a little more complicated than that. But you will need a plan. Whether you want to overcome a bad habit pattern, fear, guilt, anger, debt, or a bad relationship, you will need a plan. This book will help you with some ideas to put a plan together. It may be simple or complicated. But in all likelihood the challenge will be in putting the plan into gear, and that's the next step.

Fourth, you will need to make a commitment to obedience. Jesus told Peter to come, and Peter obeyed. He got out of the boat and he went to Jesus. Throughout this book you will find a boatload of Biblical challenges that God calls us to obey.

Fifth, be prepared for some exciting opportunities to present themselves to you. Peter walked on water, and if you will obey His call in your life through these pages, you will experience the supernatural touch of God in your life. You will become the recipient of some walking-on-water experiences too. But remember : Peter didn't walk on water until he got out of the boat.

Sixth, expect some let-downs along the way. Peter looked at the waves and began to sink. You will be distracted by the size of the obstacles as you seek to break free, and you'll get that sinking feeling. But don't despair. That's part of the journey. We're human. We don't always get it right. We take our eyes off the Lord just like Peter did.

Seventh, keep coming back to the relationship. Peter cried, "Lord, save me." It was a prayer of desperation. God loves, and responds to, desperation prayers. Just like a father hearing the screams of his distressed child, God hears yours. And He will help you and lift you up and keep you going. So, welcome aboard. I hope you will enjoy the journey and that it will be a blessing and will help you to manage and overcome your tough challenges.

Study Questions

1. What did you learn from the story of the boat in the storm?

2. What "life storms" have you experienced and how did they make you feel?

3. Which of the feelings the disciples likely experienced in their sinking ship do you most identify with, and why?

4. Can you think of a time when something good came out of a difficult situation?

5. Discuss the following statement: "It's not the size of your faith that matters, it's the size of your God, the object of your faith, that's the issue. Have confidence in Him, not in the size of your faith."

6. With which resistance factor that Peter had to overcome did you most identity?

CHAPTER 2

ADDICTIONS:

WHY DO I DO WHAT I DON'T WANT TO DO?

You can't get rid of weeds by pulling off the leaves. You have to get them out by the root. So it is with a bad habit that won't let go. There's a tough challenge: trying to stop doing things that we don't want to do. In this chapter, we will look at a seminal text in the Bible, right at the beginning of the Bible, Genesis chapter 3, that explains the root causes of surface addictions. All addictive behavior has roots. And to end the relentless habit, the roots need to be understood. But before we get to chapter three, let's discover chapter two. Genesis chapter two is the story of Adam and Eve in a garden environment, in a world of perfect obedience.

When our kids were small, we played a game where my wife wrote out a series of directional instructions and placed them in envelopes. We would then get in the car and go for a drive. The kids would take out each instruction in sequence, and tell me how far to drive, when to turn left or right, etc. The twist was that each time they told me to go left, I went right. Or when they told me to go straight, I turned left. Consequently, instead of ending up at the Ice Cream Parlour which was the intended destination, my "disobedience" led us to the back of an apartment building facing three dumpsters. The final paper in the envelope carried the moral of the game : "When we obey, we go the right way." That's the way it is with God. When we obey His Word, we go the right way. Proverbs 3:5-6 says, "Trust in the Lord with all your heart, and lean not on your own understanding; in all your ways acknowledge Him, and He will make your paths straight." When we obey, we go the right way. Jesus explains the importance of obedience in John 14:21, by equating obedience with loving Him, "He who has my commandments and obeys them, he is the one who loves Me. He who loves me will be loved by My Father, and I too will love him and will show Myself to him."

We see the results of perfect obedience in the Garden of Eden when God created Adam and Eve. They lived in a garden environment, in a state of perfect contentment and perfect obedience, and enjoyed four benefits for their obedience.

First, they experienced relational fulfillment.

The first thing God concluded after He made man was that "It is not good that the man should be alone" (Genesis 2:18). God created Adam with a capacity for relationship. He then fulfilled that capacity by creating a woman to complement Adam. Adam also enjoyed relational communion and intimacy with God. An integral component of Adam's identity and contentment was connected to relational fulfillment. God intended Adam to enjoy a harmonious, joy-filled and love-based relationship with God, with Eve --- his life partner --- and with other people. That's why so many instructions in the Scriptures are concerned with building strong relationships. We have all been born with this capacity and longing for the same relational quality.

Second, they experienced a profound sense of value.

God said, "Let us make man in Our image" (Genesis 1:26). Adam and Eve were created to have dominion over everything God created. Man was distinct among all the rest of God's creation, and he was the only creature bestowed with the honour of being made in God's image. Whatever else that means, it includes a high and profound level of value and dignity. They were image-bearers of God.

Third, they experienced a clear conscience.

Adam and Eve, in Genesis 2, knew nothing of regret, a stained conscience, guilt, or the pain of shame, making mistakes, wrong decisions, embarrassment, blushing or failure. They were innocent and had a perfectly clear conscience. The text says, "they were both naked... and were not ashamed" (2:25).

Fourth, they experienced a sense of purpose.

Adam and Eve were created for involvement. They were designed to contribute, produce, accomplish, make a difference, create, and have a sense of being useful. They were designed to work well, effectively and efficiently, free from frustration and futility. In other words, they had a sense of purpose. The text indicates that "God took the man and put him in the Garden of Eden to tend and keep it" (:15). Work was intended to produce a sense of accomplishment and the feelings associated with doing a good job. I'm not much of a carpenter, but I enjoy running a power saw across a 2x6 plank of wood. I love the smell of sawdust, and the sound of a hammer hitting a nail --- the steel kind of nail that is. A few years ago I slapped a deck together in my backyard. The night I finished it, and for a few nights afterwards, I would quietly walk over the deck, run my hand along the handrail, and eyeball the posts, evaluating the alignment. I would whisper to myself, certain that no one was around to hear, "Roy... you did a good job." We like to get to the end of a project and say, "I did a good job." I wonder if that's what God had in mind when He stepped back from His creative work on the universe at the end of each day and "saw that it was good." God intended us to produce meaningful accomplishment and to feel good when we have done a satisfactory job. That's a key ingredient in the enjoyment of contentment and a healthy identity.

These four ingredients --- relationship, value, clear conscience, and purpose --- were the results of obedience and ere perfectly experienced by Adam and Eve in Genesis chapter two. We were created with these same four longings and seek to satisfy each of them to one degree or another. In fact, every expression of disobedience constitutes an illegitimate pursuit of one of these four longings. Longings are not wrong, they're God-designed. But we go about meeting them in wrong ways. Temptation is the desire to meet legitimate longings in illegitimate ways.

So what are the consequences of disobedience? In Genesis chapter three we find a description of the tragedy of disobedience. Known as the Fall, it's the story of Adam and Eve's notorious refusal to obey God's instruction, and the choice to pursue legitimate longings in illegitimate ways. Contained in this story are the seeds of all disobedience and the profound side-effects of addictive behaviour.

Lana Bateman is an example of the pain of disobedience. She told her story in her book, *God's Crippled Children*. She exposes the depth of her pain when she describes how, at 17, she swallowed 40 pills. She writes, after waking up in hospital, "Why, why, why am I still alive? I couldn't bear the pain in my mind anymore, and I couldn't understand why a world compassionate enough to shoot a crippled horse wouldn't let a crippled human die and, at least in death, find some peace from mental agony. I fell back on my pillow and cried tears of anger, frustration, loneliness and fear. Then there were tears of emptiness and grief. The kind of grief that overcomes when one realizes she is not dead but alive. I was not free of this world and at peace, but had to stand up and face life all over again, now with the stigma of a new failure. I couldn't even succeed at dying."

What would cause a young woman at 17 years of age, to want to cause such damage to herself? How could a young woman with such promise travel such a tremendous distance and arrive at a place of such despondency? The answer lies in the description of Genesis chapter three. In this chapter we will see the six steps on the journey to addictive behaviour.

Step 1 --- Unbelief: The Root Cause of Disobedience

God operates with the currency of truth. Jesus said, "I am… the Truth…" (John 14:6). But Satan operates with the currency of lies. Jesus calls him "the father of lies" (John 8:44). Satan hates people. Jesus says that the thief (Satan) "does not come except to steal, and to kill and destroy" (John 10:10). He seeks to destroy marriages, families, spiritual lives, finances, and even your physical health. His ultimate objective for every person's life is for them to commit suicide. It is his lies and deception planted in the mind that lie at the root of all disobedience. Our culture suffers from truth decay, and it all started with Satan. Satan's conversation with Eve in Genesis chapter three reveals his three-step strategy of lies, as he engages Eve.

First, he establishes doubt. He says, "Has God indeed said, 'You shall not eat of every tree of the garden?'" (3:1). Satan ignores the fact that God has provided every tree in the garden for their enjoyment except one, and He draws Eve's attention to the one tree from which God has prohibited them from eating. That's Satan's way. He ignores all the good and wholesome things that God provides, and gets our focus on those things that God prohibits for our protection and blessing. He casts doubt on God's intent and desire to provide, and frames Him as a cosmic killjoy. He still works that same strategy today rather successfully. Many people have that exact view of God. I often hear people say, "Becoming a Christian means obeying a whole bunch of prohibitive rules." The focus is on the prohibitions rather than the multitude of blessings God intends for anyone who will walk in obedience to Him. Satan's first line of attack is always to establish doubt about the reality and goodness of God. This step finds expression in doubting the Scriptures, or the existence of God, or the goodness of God, or the value of prayer.

Second, Satan then establishes disbelief. After Eve reminds Satan about God's warning that death would follow disobedience, Satan bluntly says, "You will not surely die"

(3:4). That's blatant disbelief. Satan first establishes doubt about the veracity of God's Word, then he seeks to create unbelief. Disbelief is the natural progression from doubt. Left unattended, doubt will fester into the blister of disbelief.

Third, after casting doubt, then disbelief, Satan then moves to deception. He exchanges truth for a lie. He tells Eve, "you will be like God..." (3:5). That's exactly what Paul said in Romans 1:25 would happen when people choose disobedience : "they exchanged the truth of God for the lie". Satan begins by casting doubt on truth, then he moves to reject truth, then finally he replaces truth with lies. He convinces Eve that disobedience will be better than obedience. These are the three seeds of disobedience: doubt, disbelief, and deception. All addictive behaviour flows from erroneous thinking.

Step 2 --- Desire: The Power of Disobedience

Disobedience is attractive and compelling. The text reads, "When the woman saw that the tree was good... pleasant... and desirable... she took of its fruit..." (3:6). And not to let Adam off the hook, he took some too. Notice the attractive power of disobedience. It was good, pleasant and desirable. That's why temptation is so compelling. It's attractive. Disobedience is a powerful attraction. Why would Adam and Eve jeopardize all that they had in the Garden? It starts with doubt about God's goodness, then disbelief, then deception, and finally disobedience.

Step 3 - Lost Identity: The Consequences of Disobedience

When Adam and Eve disobeyed God, they immediately suffered a profound assault on the four issues that resulted from their obedience in Genesis 2, and the loss of their sense of identity and contentment. When we violate God's Law, we reap the same four consequences Adam and Eve suffered in Eden.

We experience relational loss

Adam and God had walked together in perfect relational intimacy, in Genesis 2. Now, as a result of disobedience, in chapter 3, Adam says, in verse 10, "I heard your voice". And Adam hides from God. God is now distant. By far, separation from God is the most catastrophic consequence of disobedience, and all other consequences flow from this cosmic interruption. There is also relational disintegration between Adam and Eve. Adam blames both God and Eve, saying, "It was that woman you gave me" (v.12). Relational disintegration transmits down to the children, when Cain kills his brother. We all long for relational fulfillment, and Adam and Eve's loss explains why we often find it to be elusive. Remember Lana? Lana never remembered being touched, kissed or held by either of her parents from infancy through adulthood. Her earliest recollection of her father was when her pet alligator bit his hand --- in rage he flushed it down the toilet. She received no affection from her mother, who couldn't tolerate anything out of place. She was raised in a house, not a home. Friends never came over. It was beautiful but cold. Her years in a house without love created a state of emotional bankruptcy. She was profoundly alone. She says, "I saw others kissing and hugging. Why didn't anyone kiss or hug me? On rare occasions I saw daddy put his arm around mother. Why didn't anyone put an arm around me? I was like a little puppy dog trying to find a lap, but every time I started to crawl in, the person stood up and walked away. I was crying, 'Please love me,' and they just kept walking away." The Book of Proverbs says, "Under three things the earth quakes, under four it cannot bear up... an unloved woman when she gets a husband." (Proverbs 30:21-23)

We experience loss of value

The second area of disintegration in the Garden was a meltdown of personal value. Adam declares, in verse 10, "I was naked". This implies that he felt shame. In chapter two, the record says, they were naked and felt no shame. There is an important distinction between guilt and shame. Guilt is a forensic term, while shame is an emotional term. Guilt describes a legal position before the law. For example, when you exceed the speed limit and get caught in a radar trap, you are legally guilty before the law. The emotional response to a position of guilt is often shame. Guilt refers to what you do, shame is an assault on who you are. Adam and Eve are still made in God's image but the confidence and sense of dignity such high esteem should bring is gone, and replaced by deep-seated shame. And we have been struggling with our sense of value ever since. One of the primary responsibilities of parents is to affirm the value and dignity of a child. To illustrate the fragility and ongoing disintegration of value and dignity, one writer said this: "Because a child perceives everything in a literal way, every expression from a parent either communicates 'you matter' or 'you're a nobody'. And Satan will use your expressions and twist them in the child's mind, and create fortresses of lies in the child's mind of who he is. Lies that will in many cases paralyze him for years.

We experience loss of innocence

Adam continues, "I was afraid" (v.10). Fear flows from shame. The conscience is now stained with shame and fear, and longs for a previously unknown concept known as forgiveness. Lana knew the feelings of unforgiveness well. Lana's mother bleached her hair white from a natural brown. At 14, she bought Lana clothes and put makeup on to make her look 25. She asks, "'Was I not acceptable as I was?' The message seemed to be that there was something wrong with me, and only with certain changes would I be accepted and loved."

Some of us go through our life with a duffel bag full of blunders. Each year brings more regrets and failures and wrong choices, and the bag gets a little fuller and a little heavier. And we long for some way to lighten the load and unload the burden, and we long for the days of innocence. And all that impacts our sense of identity.

We experience loss of purpose

The fourth disintegration was the meltdown of purpose. Adam explains, "I hid myself". In chapter 2 he was tending and keeping the garden. Now he's withdrawn from his productive work, and he's hiding. God confirms the kind of work that Adam will do as a result of his disobedience, when He says, "the ground will cause you toil ….. and bring forth thistles and thorns" (v.17-19). Work was meant to be fulfilling and productive and enjoyable, and fruitful. Now it is going to be hard and futile and a grind. One businessman reflected that truth when he said, "I feel like I'm on a treadmill, and I never feel as though I'm good enough, and no matter how fast I run I never seem to get ahead." The loss of these four capacities as a result of disobedience creates an identity crisis for Adam and Eve, and the inevitable result is emotional instability --- the next step in the journey of disobedience.

Step 4 --- Damaged Emotions: The Aftermath of Disobedience

The upshot of all these losses is that Adam and Eve feel bad --- really bad. The text says, "I was afraid". It is interesting that fear is the first negative emotion mentioned in the Bible and was the descriptive emotion Adam experienced immediately after the first act of rebellion. Fear is also the negative emotion God addresses most often in the Bible. The words "Fear not" appear over 300 times. Consider how often fear is the underlying drive behind other negative emotions, such as anger, anxiety, guilt, boredom, depression, sadness, etc. Sometimes we move beyond the feelings, and emotionally flatline. The feelings leave, and we feel nothing. The Eagles released a song in the 1970s, called *Desperado,* that described the loss of emotions. One of the lines went like this: "Losin' all your highs and lows, funny how the feelin's go away." Lana said it this way: "My response to my parents' discipline and inability to express love was a state of emotional bankruptcy." Disobedience creates damaged emotions. We don't like feeling bad. So Adam and Eve did what we all do with bad feelings. They covered and masked them and disguised them with fig leaves. That's the first evidence in the Bible of addictive behaviour.

Step 5 --- Addictive Behaviour: The Side-Effects of Disobedience

The pair of them "sewed fig leaves together and made themselves coverings" (v.7). They tried to anesthetize the pain of their shame. That is one of the most brilliant descriptions ever written to explain what we do when we feel bad. We disguise the problem with fig leaves. Fig leaves are feeble and inadequate attempts to mask bad feelings, without addressing the root reasons for the problem. There are two dominant ways we anesthetize pain. We either deaden the pain, or we pursue pleasure. Some people pursue relationships, and even marriage, to mask pain. Lana said, "I thought about my loneliness and inability to have friends, and I searched for a way to manipulate others into loving me." She said, "As a child I spent a great deal of time alone. And I see now that I gradually began to feed on that aloneness. Satan enticed me into that frame of mind. The longer I wallowed in them the more comfortable they became. Finally, I no longer controlled the aloneness and self-pity. But they controlled me." Lana met a boy at 20, and began a stormy relationship that culminated in marriage. One week before the wedding her father asked, "Why are you marrying this guy? You two don't even like each other." Marriage was a fig leaf. Lana admitted, "Because of the desperation of my needs, I could not and would not see what he saw so clearly."

Some marry to deaden the pain, others eat. They say, "My heart may be broken but my esophagus is going to have a party." Some gamble. It is ironic that the word "casino" has "sin" in the middle of the word. Casinos don't have clocks on the wall and some patrons sit for hours, paying for a few hours of painless pleasure, to mask deeper longings. Some watch pornography or engage in sexual fantasies, or have sexual affairs. Some sleep, or watch TV, or overdrink, or overspend and load up credit cards. Some keep really busy, and become workaholics. Others withdraw, from friends, from life, from responsibilities. All fig leaves.

If I anesthetize the pain, then I can ignore the disintegration of my identity and the loss of these core longings. Some of us set performance goals and expectations for ourselves and other people. We think, "If I can achieve these goals and expectations then that will satisfy the ache in my soul." One man said, "I felt like one of those guys on a stage spinning large numbers of plates on the end of poles. I was running from pole to pole to pole trying to keep all these plates spinning, terrified that one would come crashing to the floor. I got really, really tired, working so hard to hear people applaud and tell me how good a job I was doing." They are all fig leaves, designed to dull the ache of loss of these four God-given longings: relational aloneness, erosion of value, a stained conscience, and the feelings of futility. Some attempt, and others succeed with, the ultimate fig leaf, suicide. That was Lana's fig leaf. She writes, "I felt cheated out of an end to my pain, by having been thrown back into the arena and forced to suffer through a life I didn't want. Why couldn't they let the sick die?" Suicide is a fig leaf. It's simply a doorway, from one life to another. And it doesn't deal with the pain for those who are left behind.

All this, and more, represents the side effects of disobedience. We don't like bad news and so we often do one of four unhelpful things with our struggles. Some of us are in denial, and won't acknowledge the reality of what's happening because the pain isn't severe enough. Kevin Miller, in his book, *A Hunger for Healing,* said he didn't make changes until "the acid of my pain ate through the walls of my denial". If we don't deny our problem, some of us diminish the seriousness of it. We pretend it's not that serious, or rationalize it by saying everyone else is doing the same thing. Some of us blame other people by deflecting. We blame our spouse, kids, co-worker, boss or teacher. Sometimes we avoid the problem by disguising. We do what Adam and Eve did. We put on fig leaves. But none of these responses get at the root of the problem. Perhaps you have been wondering, "How did I ever get here from there?" Now you know.

So, what's the answer?

Genesis chapter three is a bleak picture, because disobedience leads to a bleak destination. Fortunately, that's the beginning of the Bible, not its end. The life, death and resurrection of the Lord Jesus Christ is the redemptive answer to all of this. The person of Jesus Christ is God's answer to the loss of the four longings we have been discussing here. Jesus Christ died on a cross, and allowed His blood to freely flow, to offer us forgiveness for all the blunders, regrets and wrong choices we have made in our lives. He affirms that your life is of infinite value and matters to God. He offers you complete forgiveness. No one lies beyond the boundaries of His ability to forgive. He gives us a redeemed relationship with God, and the power to establish new relationships with the family of God. He gives us a new purpose in life, serving Him. The story of redemption in the rest of the Bible is God's answer to the darkness of Genesis chapter three.

I sat in Roy Thompson Hall recently, watching the Toronto Symphony Orchestra --- sixty or seventy instrumentalists sitting in a series of semi circles. There were many different instruments, many different sounds, many different shapes and sizes. Every one of those instruments had a unique identity. Each one had a unique purpose, and contribution to make. All of them faced one focal point at the centre --- the conductor. When she lifted her baton, she signalled one section to play, first the percussion, then the solo piece. She even created space for a quiet, seemingly insignificant chime that was, in the pregnant silence, an expression of beauty. I wondered what would happen if everybody took their eyes off the conductor and just did their own thing. The symphony would begin to drift, and the harmony would be lost, and the beauty of diversity would become a horrible cacophony of loud, irritating noises. All because the focus was taken off the conductor.

Everyone in the Body of Christ is in the orchestra. Every one is unique and matters. Every one has a part to play and a contribution to make. Every one plays a wrong note now and again, but it's in the persistence of overcoming the wrong notes that maturity grows. Christ is the conductor. It is from Him, and Him alone, we derive our identity. When we lose our focus on Him, the symphony of the Church would begin to drift and it would lose its harmony, and the beauty of diversity would become a cacophony of loud irritating noises. Our identity flows from Him. The Apostle Paul said, "In Him we live and move and have our being" (Acts 17:28). And it's what He thinks of you that matters.

Study Questions

1. Which of the four benefits that Adam and Eve enjoyed in Genesis 2 do you find most significant, and why?

2. Have you ever experienced a period of doubt in your spiritual journey? What caused it? How did you overcome it?

3. What were your initial impressions of the chapter you have just read?

4. Which of the four losses that Adam and Eve experienced are most relevant for you, and why?

5. Discuss the following quote: "...fear is the first negative emotion mentioned in the Bible and was the descriptive emotion Adam experienced immediately after the first act of rebellion. Fear is also the negative emotion God addresses most often in the Bible. The words 'fear not' appear over 300 times. Consider how often fear is the underlying drive behind other negative emotions, such

as anger, anxiety, guilt, boredom, depression, sadness, etc."

6. Can you think of a way that you have anesthetized pain with an addictive habit?

CHAPTER 3

GUILT:

FEELIN' GOOD ABOUT FEELIN' BAD

I'll never forget the day I pumped gas and drove off without paying. I was standing at the side of my car pumping gas in the gas station. My mind was so pre-occupied, I put the pump back on it's cradle, jumped into the car, started the engine, pulled onto the street, and was several miles along the highway before I realized I hadn't paid for the gas. "What an idiot," I thought as I checked the rear view mirror for police red lights, when the most overwhelming feeling of guilt washed over me. I pulled off the highway, headed back to the station and sheepishly paid the bill with a lame excuse about being absent-minded. Most of us have felt that tide of guilt when we've made a mistake, or failed, or made a wrong choice. I could tell you about the time I walked out of Zeller's with an unpaid garden hose, but that's a story for another day. Except to say that I did go back later and pay for it.

Mind you, some people should feel guilt but don't. Like the guy who was pulled over for speeding, and profusely apologized to the police officer, claiming that he never sped, and this was totally out of character, and that it would never happen again, and so on. The officer asks for the wife's input, and she shakes her head, saying "Officer, don't believe a word of it. He has a lead foot. I keep telling him he's going to get us killed one day." The husband becomes verbally irate with his wife and gives her a piece of his mind he can't afford to lose. The horrified officer asks the woman if he always speaks to her in this manner. She responds, "Only when he's drunk."

Psalm 51 is a classic passage dealing with wrong choices, and guilt. It's written after the sordid events recorded in 2 Samuel chapters 11-13. David is taking an evening stroll on the roof of his house when he sees his neighbour, Bathsheba, taking a bath on the rooftop next door. To cut to the chase, they commit adultery and she gets pregnant. To make matters worse, David brings her husband, Uriah, home from the battle front, in the hope that he will sleep with his wife **and assume** the child is his. Uriah sleeps on the stoop of the door citing that he can't enjoy the pleasure of his wife while his men are in battle. David gets him drunk and he still sleeps in the servants quarters. Uriah was a better man drunk than David was sober. David in desperation sends him back to the battle front with a note to Joab, the commander of the forces, instructing that Uriah be placed in the fiercest part of the battle, ensuring his death. Uriah carried his own death warrant.

David is guilty of adultery, murder, and living under the pretense that he was a man of God, until Nathan the prophet confronted him, and told him a story about a wealthy king who stole a ewe lamb from his dirt poor neighbour. He asked David what he though of a guy like that. He sucked David in, and David jumped up indignant, and told Nathan what should be done to this awful king. See, David's living under the pretense of self-righteousness. Then, Nathan points his finger and says, "You are the man."

David is convicted by guilt, the baby dies, and David writes the words of Psalm 51, birthed in the context of his guilt. It's written for any who have ever felt the weight of guilt. But it is important to realize that guilt is not bad. Guilt is God's smoke alarm to let you know something's wrong. Unresolved guilt is the problem.

The Consequences of unresolved guilt

Unresolved guilt fractures fellowship with God

David develops a recurring theme, when he says, "Have mercy upon me, O God... Do not cast me away from your presence" (v.1,11). David has lost the sense of the presence of God in his life. This is the biggest problem with unresolved guilt. It interrupts fellowship with God. I remember as a kid throwing mud pies at the side of our house. A wayward mud pie hit the bathroom window, smashed it and produced a mess all over the sink and toilet in the bathroom. After I surveyed the damage and checked to see that my dad didn't hear anything, I did what any responsible, mature ten-year-old would have done : I ran away from home. All day. Didn't come back until I was really hungry. See, I didn't want to see my dad's face. And that's what guilt does to relationship. It breaks fellowship.

Unresolved guilt is constantly in your face

"My sin is always before me" (v.3). That's the way it is with guilt, isn't it? It's never far from the front burner of your memory. Like the kid who stole bubble gum from the store, and then threw it away because the guilt wouldn't allow him the pleasure of chewing it.

Unresolved guilt creates dishonesty

"You desire truth in the inward parts" (v.6). Guilt can cause you to wear a mask. Arthur Conan Doyle, the creator of Sherlock Holmes, played the rascal with some friends when he sent each of them an anonymous telegram with the simple message, "All is discovered; flee at once." And the revealing end of the story is that each of them immediately took the telegram's advice, and left the country.

Unresolved guilt makes you miserable

David has lost his joy, and says, "Make me hear joy and gladness... Restore to me the joy of Your salvation" (v.8a,12). One man expresses the sorrow guilt produces, when he wrote this:

"I'm 31 years old and I have failed. I feel badly. I have no hope for my future. Often I go home and cry but there's no one holding me when I cry. Nobody cares. Nothing changes and I continue to fail. I'm stressed emotionally and I feel I'm on the verge of a collapse. Something is very wrong. But I feel so hurt and embittered that I can scarcely react or relate to others anymore. I feel as if I'm going to have to sit out the rest of my life in the penalty box."

Unresolved guilt drains you emotionally and physically

David reveals the physical impact of guilt when he writes, "that the bones you have broken may rejoice" (v.8b). Sometimes my kids will wrestle me to the ground --- all of them on top, from the heaviest to the lightest. When they are stacked, you just don't move. It's all I can do to whisper, "Get off me." David may have felt a little like that. Perhaps he feels like God was sitting on him, and he feels crushed.

Unresolved guilt paralyses your ministry

David makes an interesting request. He says, "Do good in your good pleasure to Zion; Build the walls of Jerusalem..." (v.18b). You see, David has been tearing Jerusalem apart. He's not been serving and bringing benevolent contribution to the people. He's asking God to do what he knows he's not been doing for the city. Guilt sometimes robs you of the ability to bring benevolence and blessing and encouragement and love into the lives of other people.

Notice, all this guilt that David is experiencing is Holy Spirit-induced guilt. There is a big difference between true and false guilt.

The source of true guilt is the Holy Spirit. The source of false guilt is the flesh and/or Satan.

The focus of true guilt will be on specific sin that needs to be confessed and repented of. The focus of false guilt will be on your identity and value as a person.

The result of true guilt will be genuine humility. The result of false guilt will be shame.

The cure for true guilt is confession and repentance. The remedy for false guilt is managing the pain through masking and avoiding.

The cure for guilt

Be Well Acquainted With God's Inclination

Before dealing with guilt, it is important to understand God's inclination towards guilt and offence. Here is an important question. What kind of a Father is God? Is He a Father who never grants second chances, who doesn't tolerate failure, who condemns and demeans and is never pleased and always expects more and who always seems to be mad at you and doles out punishment at every turn? Or is He a wise and loving and gracious Father who leads and guides and teaches and protects and provides and is kind and merciful and gives second chances and who disciplines fairly and firmly and redemptively? So which will it be? Notice David's words: "Have mercy upon me, O God, according to your lovingkindness; according to the multitude of your tender mercies..." (v.1). God is a forgiving, gracious, merciful, kind and loving God who gives second chances. That's His nature.

Be Broken

Notice David's awareness of the depth of his wrongdoing. He says, "my transgressions...my iniquity... my sin. For I acknowledge my transgressions... Against You, You only, have I sinned, and done this evil in Your sight... I was brought forth in iniquity, and in sin my mother conceived me…" (v.1-5). When our kids were smaller, a common routine often took place in the back seat of the car. It would go something like this : "Mum, he's looking at me", to which the other would respond, "No, I'm not." That's what you call denial. Then she would say, "Mum, he's touching me." And the standard reply would be, "It was an accident." That's what you call defending. Then she would say, "Mum, he hit me", to which he would respond, "It was just a tap." That's called diminishing. Then it would go on, "Mum, he's nipping me," and he would reply, "She nipped me first." That's what you call deflecting blame. This is where mum gets spiritual and begins to pray, "O Heavenly Father, help me," and she throws a blanket over the head of child #1, and tells him to go to sleep. After a few moments of silence we hear, "Mummmm, she's looking at me." That's what you call the disguised response. Camouflaged. We do that with sin. We deny it and say it's not happening. We defend it and make excuses for it. We diminish it and say it's not so bad. We deflect it and blame it on other people. We disguise it and camouflage it and pretend it's not happening. David doesn't do any of that, He calls his offence a transgression --- breaking God's law. He calls it sin --- missing the mark. And he calls it iniquity --- a perversion of God's plan and purposes.

I learned to water-ski the first time I visited Canada. After trying a few times to get up, my cousin, Wes, set me on the front of his skis and said, "Don't fight the skis. Wherever they go, you go. For if you stiffen up and try to force the skis to go in a direction other than where I want them to go, you're going to be fighting against me. And if that happens there's going to be trouble." In other words, you must be broken and surrendered to the will of the skis. This is the way to humility. And humility is the way to power. Jesus said, "Apart from Me you can do nothing" (John 15:5).

Roy Hession, in his little book, *The Calvary Road*, said,

If we are to come into this right relationship with Him, the first thing we must learn is that our wills must be broken to His will. To be broken is the beginning of revival. It is painful. It is humiliating, but it is the only way. It is being 'Not I, but Christ." And a "C" is a bent "I". The Lord Jesus cannot live in us fully and reveal Himself through us until the proud self within us is broken. This simply means that the hard unyielding self, which justifies itself, wants its own way, stands up for its rights, and seeks its own glory, at last bows its head to God's will, admits it's wrong, gives up its own way to Jesus, surrenders its rights and discards its own glory --- that the Lord Jesus might have all and be all. In other words it is dying to self and self attitudes.

Be Forgiven

David says, "Blot out my transgressions. Wash me thoroughly from my iniquity, and cleanse me from my sin… Purge me with hyssop, and I shall be clean; Wash me and I shall be whiter than snow… Hide your face from my sins, and blot out all my iniquities… Deliver me from the guilt of bloodshed." (v.1,2,7,9,14). Romans 8:1 says, "There is therefore now no condemnation against you". Jesus didn't come to rub your mistakes in. He came to rub them out. He said, "I didn't come to condemn the world; I came to save it" (John 3:17). He was nailed to the cross so that I could quit nailing myself to the cross.

How often do you think of a bill that's not been paid yet? It's on your mind all the time. How often do you think about a bill once it's been paid? You forget about it. When Jesus was on the cross He said, "It is finished." Tetelastai. That was an accounting word. When a bill was settled, the creditor would stamp the word "tetelastai" across the invoice --- "Paid in full". That's the word Jesus spoke on the cross: "Tetelastai" --- "Paid in full". There's no regret, failure, mistake or wrong choice in your life that lies beyond the boundary of God's forgiveness. Imagine a child breaking a dish, and sobbing, and saying "I'm so sorry." And you say, "It's okay. It's only a dish. Dry up the tears." And next day the child is sobbing again and you say, "What's wrong?" And the child says, "You're still angry with me about that dish yesterday." How would you feel? You'd say, "I told you it's okay. You're forgiven." And the child says, "I don't believe you." How would it feel to know your child doesn't trust your word? God said, "If you confess your sin, He is faithful and just and will forgive you your sin and cleanse you from all unrighteousness" (1 John 1:9). You need to take Him at His word.

Be Repentant

Repentance simply means to turn around from a wrong direction. It means to start afresh. It means to stop doing wrong and start doing right. David carries the repentant heart when he says, "Create in me a clean heart, O God, and renew a steadfast spirit within me... The sacrifices of God are a broken spirit, a broken and a contrite heart..." (v. 10, 17).

If I come to your house for dinner and swipe the silver, and get caught and profusely apologize and beg for forgiveness, let's assume you're the forgiving type, and you let it go. But imagine if, the next time I'm over, I swipe the pictures off the wall, and get caught and apologize and beg for forgiveness, you'll be more skeptical that the remorse is really real. Why? Because there has been no repentance.

It's not enough to simply say, "I'm sorry." There must be a behavioural change. You have to stop sinning. And that requires a changed heart. That's why David says, "Create in me a clean heart." Guilt from the past is lifted when there is godly sorrow and repentance in the present.

Be Redemptive And Repair The Damage When Possible

David wants to make amends when he says, "Then I will teach transgressors Your ways, and sinners shall be converted to You… and my tongue shall sing aloud of Your righteousness. O Lord, open my lips, and my mouth shall show forth Your praise…" (v.13,14,15). David couldn't change the past. He couldn't go back and make the adultery and Uriah's murder not happen. Sometimes you can't repair the damage. But you repair it when you can. And when you can't, then you seek to redemptively contribute where possible. You can't change the past but you can alter your future. That's what David is saying here. "I want to be a redemptive contributor in the days ahead."

Be Hopeful For The Future

"Then You shall be pleased with the sacrifices of righteousness…" (v.19). God is the God of the second chance. He will be pleased with David again. In Acts 13:22, David is called a man after God's own heart, because the inclinations of God's heart is toward loving kindness and tender mercy and love and grace and forgiveness and second chances. I came across the following prayer that gets at the heart of God's inclinations:

"God, when I'm wretched and weak You love me

When I'm steady and strong You love me

When I'm very right or terribly wrong You love me

When I talk too much or laugh too loud

or sob too long You love me

When I'm quiet and serene You love me

When I obey You, You love me

When I insist on my own way You love me

When I fail to put You first, You love me

When I come running back to You, You love me

I need not beg You to love me

For You who are love cannot exist without loving me

And yet this very day dear God, I have no real

assurance of Your love at all.

I wonder why."

"Beloved child, the fact remains I love you anyway."

Study Questions

1. Can you think of a time when you felt really guilty? What was the cause?

2. What was your first impression of the chapter on guilt?

3. Which of the consequences of guilt are most relevant and that you identity with?

4. Talk about how often false guilt is a part of your life.

5. Talk about how realistic and helpful the cure is for guilt.

CHAPTER 4

MONEY:

SIX POTHOLES ON THE ROAD TO BUILDING WEALTH

Your money matters to God. God talks about money in the Bible as much as He does about Heaven. He has written in the Scriptures all you need to know about how to build wealth. The Scriptures talk about how to make money, how to save it, view it, spend it, give some of it away, and how to protect it. The Scriptures talk about how to avoid being enslaved by money, and how to order and manage it so that you can enjoy it. God intended money to be a blessing, not a curse. Unfortunately, when we don't handle money well, it can become a curse. Some people worry about money, and stress over it so much they can never enjoy the blessing of it. Money pressures are often cited as a major cause in marriage breakdowns. God's money principles properly applied will build wealth. When these principles are neglected and violated, the consequences are like financial potholes. Potholes are hard on a car, and make driving dangerous. When one of your wheels drops into a pothole, it can rip the muffler right off. Potholes break tie-rod ends and shock absorbers. Sometimes you'll see a sign on the side of the road warning you to drive carefully and watch for potholes ahead. I want to show you six financial potholes that you need to watch out for. These six potholes can rip the wheels right off your financial bus, if you hit enough of them, often enough. Let's talk about them, and see which of them you recognize.

Pothole #1 --- Debt

We live in a society of "Buy now, and pay for the rest of your life". Someone said, "I'd be happy to pay as I go, if only I could finish paying for where I have already been." Someone said, "We buy things we don't need, with money we don't have, to impress people we don't like." Everyone borrows --- even, or especially, governments. Our instantaneous lifestyle conditions us to want everything now. Rather than exercise the discipline to save and wait, we spend and pay interest, and by the time it's paid for, it's ready to be replaced. The Bible says, "Owe no man anything, except the debt of love" (Romans 13:8). There are three problems with debt. First, debt makes you a slave. The Bible says, "The borrower is servant to the lender" (Proverbs 22:7). The greater the debt load, the deeper the bondage. The larger the debt, the lesser your options and freedom. The second problem with debt is that it can jeopardize your reputation. The Bible says, "The wicked borrow and do not repay" (Psalm 37:21). When you lack the means to repay a debt, character is lost, and that is a high price to pay. The third problem with debt is that it exposes you to serious loss. The Bible says, "If you lack the means to pay, your very bed will be snatched from under you" (Proverbs 22:27). You should never risk what you are not prepared to lose. It's a lot easier to get into debt than to get out. And the longer you maintain a habit of carrying debt, the more difficult it is to reverse the habit. If you have been carrying consumer debt for more than five years, the odds are that you will practice the habit of carrying debt the rest of your life. The cost of carrying personal debt is enormous, especially over a lifetime. If you pay the short-term price of getting out of debt, and cultivate a lifestyle of "pay as you go", you will save yourself likely hundreds of thousands of dollars over the course of your life. The only wise use of a credit card is when you pay off the total balance every month and pay zero interest. Every month a balance is left on a credit card, you are moving further into the territory of unmanageable debt. The challenge of getting out of unmanageable debt is formidable, but not insurmountable :

Step one. You need to take a complete inventory of exactly how much you owe.

Step two. Turn off the credit tap and put a padlock on it. If you are in unmanageable debt, you cannot creep out of debt. You cannot tame the debt dragon. You have to kill it. You have to cut off its head. You have to eliminate the access to debt. If you have credit cards, you need to take a pair of scissors and bravely cut them up. If you have an overdraft protection, you need to pay off the overdue balance and cancel the protection. Here's the law of unmanageable debt: "if you have access to credit you will use it, but if you don't, you won't". This is why people go to a credit counseling company, and get all their loans consolidated, but a year later they have more credit card debt because they didn't cut off their access to a credit card.

This simple principle is the reason why many people can never get free of debt. Because they can't find the courage to cut off access to credit. They fear that they won't be able to pay the bills, if they don't have access to the credit reserve. They use credit as a safety net. The only way to overcome this fear is to understand that if the debt continues to grow, and the minimum monthly payments can't be met, then credit access will be denied by the loan company eventually anyway. Far better to cut access off voluntarily with a strategic redemptive plan, than to have it imposed on you.

Step three. Pay down the debt. Contact all creditors and make manageable monthly payment arrangements at the lowest interest possible. Talking to your bank about a consolidated loan may be helpful here. One low interest rate is better than several high interest credit card rates. This also creates one lower monthly payment, rather than several higher payments.

Pothole #2 --- Living Paycheck to Paycheck

If debt is the biggest pothole on the road to building wealth, spending everything you earn every month is the second. When you spend everything you earn, nothing is being saved. God's Word says, "He who gathers money little by little makes it grow" (Proverbs 13:11). There's a number of things to note about that verse.

First, God's plan is that we "gather", or save, money. God doesn't want you to live paycheck to paycheck and spend everything you earn. His plan is for you to spend less than you earn. And the only way to do that is to pay yourself first.

Second, God's design is to build wealth slowly and consistently. Cultivating the habit of making regular payments to your own savings account is far more important than the actual amount you save. Some people make the mistake of trying to save more than they can afford, then they dip back into the savings for monthly expenses. The first savings withdrawal is the hardest, then it becomes easier to make the next withdrawal, and pretty soon you're back to square one. This is truly discouraging. Far better to start small, and not miss. Setting percentage targets is helpful here. Saving 10% of your total take-home salary is a commonly suggested amount to save. But you may not be able to save that much at this point, so begin with five, or three, or one percent. The habit is more important than the actual amount.

Third, God intends for your wealth to grow. He wants you to build wealth. But building and growing wealth implies work and diligence and faithfulness and obedience. God never intended you to grow your wealth by "get-rich-quick" schemes, or by winning the lottery. I remember a fella saying to me one day, "If God wants me to win the lottery, He still expects me to go buy the ticket." In his desire to illustrate the importance of our responsibilities while trusting the Lord, he was wrong. God would never want you to win the lottery, because that's not the way He designed wealth to be built.

Pothole #3 --- Stinginess

God intended money to be a blessing, not a curse. He intends for you to build wealth, and for you to enjoy the blessing that money can provide. However, God never intended for us to exclusively spend our money on ourselves. That's stinginess. God wants us to give away a portion of our resources to worthy causes. He promises that if we will be generous with our money, and not stingy, He will reward us. The Apostle Paul said, "He who sows sparingly will also reap sparingly, and he who sows bountifully will also reap bountifully" (2 Corinthians 9:6). Jesus makes the same point in Luke 6:38, when He says, "Give, and it will be given to you. A good measure, pressed down, shaken together and running over will be put into your bosom. For with the same measure that you use, it will be measured back to you." Sometimes the reason money is tight is that we're tight with our money. Since all that we have comes from God's gracious Hand, we are to show our appreciation and gratitude by giving back to the Lord's work. The Bible says, "There is one who scatters yet increases more. And there is one who withholds more than is right, but it leads to poverty" (Proverbs 11:24). Proverbs says, "Honour the Lord with your possessions and with the firstfruits of all your increase, then your barns will be filled with plenty, and your vats will overflow with new wine." (3:9,10). Notice we are to honour the Lord with the "firstfruit". That means the amount we give to the Lord should be our first priority, not what's left over.

Here are some questions and answers about how to give.

How much should I give? You decide. 2 Corinthians 9:7 says, "let each one give as he purposes in his heart…". So you decide how much you want to give as an expression of your gratitude.

Why should I give? Because of God's grace and kindness towards you. Paul goes on, in verse 7, "Give… not grudgingly or of necessity; for God loves a cheerful giver." No one likes to take a gift from someone who really doesn't want to give it; neither does God. This helps to answer the previous question --- give whatever amount you can give cheerfully.

To whom should I give? Whatever worthy causes you deem worthy is an appropriate target of your giving. However, the New Testament teaches a pattern of giving to the Lord's work by giving to the local church, or set of local churches. (See 1 Corinthians 16:1-4; 2 Corinthians 8:1-7). So it would be appropriate for you to give first to the local church where you are fed spiritually and where you serve. Then, it would be appropriate to give to other worthy causes that are working to spread the Gospel of the Lord Jesus Christ and expand the Kingdom around the world.

Pothole #4 --- Dishonesty

God intended money to be made honestly. The Bible describes many ways money is made dishonestly. Bad

business practice is a dishonest form of making money. Proverbs says, "Dishonest scales are an abomination to the Lord, but a just weight is his delight" (11:1). It is important in business practice to be fair and just. Stealing is a dishonest form of making money. Paul says, "Let him who stole steal no longer, but rather let him labour, working with his hands what is good, that he may have something to give him who has need" (Ephesians 4:28). Don't take what isn't yours. Stealing can take the form of not paying your taxes. The Bible mentions three problems with dishonest gain.

First, it disappears. "Wealth gained by dishonesty will be diminished" (Proverbs 13:11). People who are dishonest with money often never learn how to build wealth, and no matter how much they earn, there never seems to be enough.

Second, dishonest money doesn't produce contentment. The Bible says, "Bread gained by deceit is sweet to a man, but afterward his mouth will be filled with gravel" (Proverbs 20:17).

Third, dishonest money will bring judgment. James, talking about people who make their money dishonestly, says "Come now, you rich, weep and howl for your miseries that are coming upon you" (5:1). Dishonest income can lead to severe consequences, especially when caught. Heavy fines, incarceration or job loss far outweigh any advantage made by dishonest gain. So, be sure to make your money honestly. Minimum wage made honestly is better by far than double the rate, if it's dishonest.

Pothole #5 --- Carelessness

The Bible mentions a number of ways that money and property can be used carelessly.

First, lack of understanding and appreciation for the source of all your resources produces carelessness.

All our resources come from God's gracious Hand. The Bible says, "Every good and perfect gift comes from above" (James 1:17). David said in 1 Chronicles 29:12, "Both riches and honour come from You...". Everything belongs to God and ultimately comes from His hand. Jesus said, in the Lord's prayer, "Give us this day our daily bread". That means we are to be dependent on Him for even the basic necessities of life. He is the reason we have a job. He gave us the health and abilities to hold down a job and be able to do the work. He is the one who keeps us working and gives us the ability to bring home a paycheck, in spite of a poor economy.

Second, neglect of property is a form of carelessness.

Proverbs says, "I went by the field of the lazy man...and there it was, all overgrown with thorns... A little sleep, a little folding of the hands to rest, so shall your poverty come like a prowler" (24:30-34). When property is neglected, the value of the property depreciates faster. This also reflects a lack of appreciation for the property you have. So take good care of your clothes, car, home, etc.

Third, not keeping accurate records is a form of carelessness.

Proverbs says, "Be diligent to know the state of your flocks, and attend to your herds; for riches are not forever" (27:23-24). This was written in an agricultural society. Flocks and herds were their resources. And they were to keep careful scrutiny over what they owned. They knew exactly what they earned and what they owed. Some people take an ostrich approach to finances and become so overwhelmed by bills that they stop opening the envelopes, and just drop them immediately into the recycling bin.

The application for us would be to keep an accurate budget. A budget is a careful accounting of how much money comes into the house each month and how it goes out. Less should always go out than what comes in. If you've never operated on a budget before, here's an easy way to get started.

1.Take a sheet of paper and write at the top of the page, the amount of money that you bring home each month.

2.Down the left side of the page write all the things that you spend that money on each month, along with the amount you spend. This should be a comprehensive list which should include even once-a-year expenses, divided into 12 monthly amounts. While everyone's list will be unique, be sure to include the following: rent/mortgage, heating, hydro, phone, cable, food, insurance (car, house, life), pet food and expenses, RRSP, car payment, gas and maintenance, clothes, pocket money, entertainment, debt repayment, vacation, pension fund, emergency fund, savings, charitable giving. Nothing is too small for this list. If you buy a coffee each day, that's $50 for coffee per month. If you spend more than you take in, you need to make some major adjustments.

3.Set up a series of envelopes designated for appropriate budget items, and keep in a safe and secure place. For example, you could have envelopes for groceries, gas money, entertainment, charitable giving, pocket money, clothes, pet food, etc. Money can then be kept in these envelopes each month until needed. Emergency fund, RRSP, vacation fund, and savings should be set up in appropriate bank accounts.

Fourth, unplanned impulse buying, or spontaneous purchases, is a form of carelessness.

There's nothing wrong with spontaneous purchases, so long as you plan for them. You need to know that you can afford them. The problem is with impulsive buying that hasn't been planned for and isn't affordable. So, if you're an impulse buyer, you need to include a line in your budget for spontaneity. This way, you can budget an amount to spend impulsively without feeling guilty about it.

Fifth, investing money in untrustworthy schemes is a form of carelessness.

Proverbs says, "He who chases fantasies lacks judgment... and will have his fill of poverty" (12:11; 28:19). Investing money in untrustworthy schemes is usually motivated by a desire to get rich quick. As we have already noted, God's plan to build wealth is by consistently saving money, bit by bit.

Finally, we handle money carelessly when we pay for things we shouldn't be paying for.

That's what you call waste. Incurring speeding tickets is a result of careless driving. Paying more for hydro is a result of not turning off lights.

Pothole #6 --- Obsession

The Bible says, "the love of money is the root of all evil" (1 Timothy 6:10). That's obsessing over money. Jesus said in Matthew 6:21, "Where your treasure is, there your heart will be also." If money is your treasure, that's where your heart will be. When money is an obsession it has become an idol, and occupies the throne of your life. In Matthew 6:25-34, Jesus teaches about the problem of worry, and that comes immediately after his teaching on storing up treasures in heaven. Worrying about money is a sign that you are obsessing about money, and that money has become an idol. Most people don't obsess over money for money's sake, but rather for what money can provide --- a nice house, nice car, nice things, nice holidays, nice security, nice retirement, nice reputation, nice feeling of self worth. Here are some things worth considering when you obsess over money.

1. Money doesn't satisfy.

The Bible says, "Whoever loves money never has money enough. Whoever loves wealth is never satisfied with his income" (Ecclesiastes 5:10).

2. Money is temporal.

"Cast but a glance at riches and they are gone, for they

will surely sprout wings and fly off to the sky like an eagle" (Proverbs 23:5).

3. Love of money produces agitation.

"Better a little with the fear of the Lord, than great wealth with turmoil" (Proverbs 15:16). When people value property over people, relationships are strained. I remember watching a guy and his wife pulling into a dock with a beautiful 32-foot sailboat. As they docked, evidently she did something wrong with one of the ropes and he gave her a piece of his mind that, frankly, he couldn't afford to lose. Possessions are more important than people sometimes. You either possess possessions, or you're possessed by possessions. Haddon Robinson said, "Money is like flypaper. The fly lands on the flypaper and says, 'This is my flypaper.' Pretty soon the flypaper says, 'This is my fly.'"

4. Obsessing about money can produce a lack of wisdom.

"A man with an evil eye hastens after riches and does not consider that poverty will come upon him" (Proverbs 28:22).

5. Obsessing about money can destroy your health.

"Do not wear yourself out to get rich" (Proverbs 23:4).

6. Obsessing about money means money is your #1 treasure.

"No man can serve two masters" (Matthew 6:24); "Seek first the Kingdom of God and His righteousness…" (Matthew 6:33); "Give me neither poverty nor riches, but give me only my daily bread. Otherwise I may have too much and disown You… or I may become poor and steal" (Proverbs 30:8,9).

7. Obsessing about money can destroy your faith.

The Apostle Paul warned that, "Those who desire to be rich fall into temptation and a snare, and into many foolish and harmful lusts which drown men in destruction and perdition. For the love of money is a root of all kinds of evil, for which some have strayed from the faith in their greediness, and pierced themselves through with many sorrows" (1 Timothy 6:9,10).

A man in our church ran his own business. One day a client placed a sizable order and attached a set of conditions that would have compromised my friend's integrity and Christian testimony. His response to the client was, "I can't do that. I would still like your business but I can't do that. My integrity and testimony and character are more important to me than the profits I would make from your order. Money is not my obsession. Loving God, and pleasing Him, matters more to me than making money." His client took his business elsewhere, and he lost the order. Other Christian businessmen have not been willing to pay that price. Making money mattered so much they got tempted, and trapped, and then lusted for more, and they got swallowed up. Worst of all, men and women who start out loving God sacrifice too much in the pursuit of money and pay dearly when they lose their testimony and, sadly, their faith.

8. Obsessing about money blinds you to ultimate realities.

Money, and the things money can buy, are not the most important things in life. The most important things in life are not things. And the most important things are monetarily free, but they're not cheap. Only two things will last forever --- God's Word, and people. Money doesn't last. The Book of Proverbs says, "Riches do not profit in the day of wrath, but righteousness delivers from death" (11:4). Far wiser it is to invest your life in that which will last forever.

Study Questions

1. Which of the six potholes do you think is most dangerous and why?

2. What do you think of the idea that God intended money to be a blessing, not a curse?

3. Why do you think God cares so much about how you handle your money?

4. Which of the potholes do you find hardest to avoid and why?

CHAPTER 5

MARRIAGE:

PERMANENT OR EXPERIMENT?

Anyone who says that the Bible is dull, boring or irrelevant hasn't read Mark 10:1-11. Challenging, yes. Boring, never. The Pharisees, in verse 2, came and tested Jesus by asking, "Is it lawful for a man to divorce his wife?" There's a question that could just as easily be asked in our own culture, without any need for cross-cultural translation. In that one question, we learn much about the state of marriage in the culture of the first century.

Divorce rates were skyrocketing.

That's why they're asking the question. Divorce was a front-burner issue of the day. Marriages were breaking down. Divorce was common even among spiritual leaders, especially among Pharisees. Divorce was kicking the teeth out of marriage.

Divorce was controversial.

Matthew, in 19:3, describing the same event, adds a bit more information to the question the Pharisees ask. "Is it lawful for a man to divorce his wife *for just any reason*?" One of the principles of interpretation is the need to understand the cultural context. That means sometimes you need to understand the cultural context before you can understand what is meant. For example, I heard a guy on the radio recently saying that his mother was learning how to text, and learning the meaning of all the abbreviations, such as LOL which means, of course, "Laugh Out Loud". But she thought it meant "lots of love". So she texted her friend who just lost her husband and said, "Sorry to hear about your husband. LOL."

When you see the letters "LOL" you need to know the cultural context in order to understand what it means. So, in Matthew 19, why would they ask, "Can a guy get a divorce for just any reason?" What was the cultural context? There was a big debate in the culture about divorce, splitting people into two camps. If you went into a barber shop in that culture, it would be guaranteed that all the people in the shop would be split into one of these two camps. One camp would be really loose on divorce and would say that a guy could get a divorce for any reason. The other camp was tight on divorce and said you could only divorce for a select few reasons. A fella by the name of Rabbi Hillel had died about twenty years before this and his liberal teaching on divorce was the popular notion. Rabbi Hillel said, "For any reason, unload that woman." John MacArthur notes that, "Under this view, you could divorce your wife for burning your dinner, for spinning around so that somebody saw her ankles, for letting her hair down (not metaphorically, but literally), for speaking to a man, or for making a negative comment about your mother, or if you found someone else that you preferred. And you were obligated to divorce her if she was infertile." That was the reigning view.

Divorce had infected the spiritual community.

Notice that the text says this is a test. It's a trap. At least the Pharisees think it's a trap. They're trying to trip Jesus into saying something that will turn the crowd against Him. They don't really care about the answer. They aren't really interested in knowing whether divorce is right or wrong, lawful or unlawful, in God's eyes. They don't want truth here, they want a trap. Their minds were made up a long time ago. They just want to see which camp Jesus will line up with, because if they can do that, then one camp will love Him and the other will hate Him. They're trying to split the vote. They don't care about divorce because divorce is in the spiritual community, all the way up to the top of the spiritual ladder and the religious leaders are doing it along with the rest of the culture.

Scripture is being used to rationalize divorce.

Jesus answers them in verse 3, "What did Moses command you?" That's an interesting response. He answers a question with a question. Now He's setting them up. The hunted has become the hunter. He turns their attention back to Scripture. What a marvellous illustration for resolving a problem. Let's get beyond what the culture says and let's go back to what the Scripture says. So they said, "Moses permitted a man to write a certificate of divorce and to dismiss her." So there it is: Scriptural grounds for getting a divorce. Except that Jesus neutralizes their answer in verse 5 : "Jesus answered and said to them, 'because of the hardness of your heart he wrote you this precept.'" They missed the point of Moses' use of a certificate of divorce. Divorce is caused by a hardness of heart, and in Moses' day, hearts were so hardened that divorce was running rampant and Moses instituted the certificate of divorce to suppress the volume of divorces that were taking place, not to encourage them. They were misinterpreting Scripture in order to justify divorce.

Divorce was caused by hardness of heart.

James would agree with Jesus' assessment of the core cause of divorce. He says. "What causes fights and quarrels among you?...Don't they come from your desires that battle within you? You want something and don't get it." (James 4:1-2) Hard heartedness is wanting something really badly and not being able to get it. And James says that leads to killing and coveting and quarrelling and fighting... and ultimately divorce.

So there's the state of marriage back in the day. Sounds familiar, doesn't it? Now, let's see Jesus' response. We're going to tackle the rest of this passage through two lenses. First, positively, then negatively. First, we'll take it from Jesus' perspective on marriage, then from Jesus' perspective on divorce. The first thing Jesus does, is to establish :

The Origin of Marriage.

"But at the beginning of creation, God made them male and female" (v.6). Marriage was God's idea. He said way back in Genesis 2, "It is not good for a man to be alone." (v.18) Elsewhere God says, "He who finds a wife finds a good thing" (Proverbs 18:22). In Ecclesiastes chapter 4, Solomon wrote, "Two are better than one, for when they lie down they keep each other warm on a cold winter's night" (I added that last bit about a cold winter's night). Then Jesus explains :

The Plan for marriage

Notice God made them male and female. God's plan for marriage was one man and one woman together for life. Not two men, or two women, or one man and three women. Then Jesus describes :

The Blueprint for Marriage

Now, Jesus gets into the guts of what makes a marriage work. This is like taking the head of an engine and exposing the pistons, valves, and all that makes an engine work. But this is much less complicated. In fact, a successful, pleasurable joy-filled marriage has three basic ingredients. Very simple. Not easy to implement, but simple to understand. And Jesus mentions all three.

The first ingredient is loyalty. Verse 7 : "For this reason a man will leave his father and mother and be joined to his wife." The fifth commandment says, "Honour your father and you mother." In your childhood years your parents are the most important people in your life. They should be the target of your greatest loyalty. No one should be more important than them. But the moment you marry, you cut the apron strings and your loyalty transfers from them to your spouse. Your marriage partner now becomes the most important person in your world. No one else in the world can compete for your loyalty. Not parents, not children, not work, not friends. The greatest gift parents can give their children, and the greatest security and safety children can experience, is a mom and a dad who are so loyal to one another that no one, or nothing, can come between them.

The second ingredient of a successful marriage is exclusivity. Jesus says, "and be joined to his wife". The sexual union is the outward physical expression of the mystical union experienced in the marriage relationship. In 1 Corinthians 6:16, Paul says, "Don't you know that he who unites himself with a harlot is one with her in body. For it is said, 'the two will become one flesh'." The sexual union was designed to be an exclusive relationship between the husband and wife, never to be compromised by an outside third party.

Then, the third ingredient of a successful marriage is commitment. Jesus goes on to say, "and the two shall become one flesh. So they are no longer two but one". The two become one in two senses. First, when two people get married, they become one instantly, before God. In a second sense, they grow into oneness over a long period of time. A lifetime together. So much so, that some say, "I don't know where I end, and she begins." That only happens because of a lifelong commitment to obey all the instructions God gives to a husband and wife, designed to build a God-honouring union --- Instructions like love, forgiveness, kindness, servanthood, honour, respect, etc.

Finally, Jesus wraps up His teaching on marriage by talking about the permanence of marriage.

Verse 9 : "Therefore what God has joined together, let man not separate." Marriage is for life. Build a marriage on the bedrock principles of God's Word, and your marriage will withstand hurricane force winds. Jesus said it this way at the end of the Sermon on the Mount : "The one who hears my words and obeys them, is like a wise man who built his house on the rock and when the wind howled and the rain came and the floods rose and beat against his house, it stood firm." (Matthew 7:24-27)

So there we have Jesus' teaching on the magnificent wonder of marriage. Now let's go back to the beginning and unpack the text from a different perspective. Let's see Jesus' teaching on divorce, because that was the subject matter of the question Jesus was asked, that started this whole discussion. Remember, the Pharisees had asked, "Is it lawful for a man to divorce his wife?" Now let's examine Jesus' answer.

Divorce is man's plan. Verses 3-6. Remember what Jesus had said about Moses and divorce? It was because of the hardness of their hearts. Then He said, "It was not so from the beginning." God is in the marriage business. Man designed the divorce business.

Divorce shatters the divine plan. Verses 6-8. Remember Jesus' blueprint for marriage? Loyalty, exclusivity, commitment. He's answering their question. Divorce shatters this blueprint.

Divorce shreds what God put together. Verse 9 says, "What God has joined, let not man separate." Divorce shreds. What happens if you pull something apart that is permanently glued? Imagine tearing apart two pieces of cardboard that have been glued together with strong adhesive. They shred. Each part leaves debris on the other.

Well, the disciples can't believe what Jesus has just said. This raises a ton of questions. What about people in bad marriages, or are already divorced, or those who are remarried? Surely Jesus can't be serious. There has to be some exceptions. But Jesus hasn't given any wiggle room. So in verse 10, they come in to the house and they ask Him to elaborate. And here's what He says in verse 11. "So He said to them, 'Whoever divorces his wife and marries another, commits adultery against her.'" Well I think you could have heard a pin drop at this point. The disciples are wishing they'd never asked. Jesus has just dropped a bombshell.

The fourth thing he says about divorce is that divorce produces adultery. Verses 11-12. He goes on, just in case the women think they're off the hook. "And if she divorces her husband and marries another man, she commits adultery." Jesus couldn't be clearer. Divorce is never permitted by God. Ever.

Furthermore, in Matthew 5:32, Jesus adds this, "And anyone who marries a woman so divorced commits adultery." So let's summarize. If a man divorces and remarries he commits adultery; if a woman divorces and remarries she commits adultery; and when they remarry they cause the third party person they get married to, to commit adultery. So when divorce occurs, it sets in motion a whole chain reaction of adulterous acts.

So Jesus has presented four reasons why divorce is wrong. There are no grounds for divorce.

Jesus' teaching on divorce stuns the disciples. They can't believe what He's said. Matthew 19:10 records the disciples' reaction. "If such is the case with a man and his wife it is better not to marry." This clearly demonstrates that the disciples understand clearly Jesus' position on divorce. And their assessment is also the world's view. If there's no trapdoor, no exit strategy, it's better not to get married. When I do a wedding, I ask couples if they promise to never seek to end their marriage in a court of law by divorce. And I always get grief from somebody. They'll rant, "How can you ask young people to promise to marry for life? They don't know. That's ridiculous." That's exactly what the disciples meant.

Now, if you have read anything about Jesus' teaching on divorce, you're thinking, "What about the exception clause?" Well, I'm glad you asked. There is a clause in Matthew 5 and Matthew 19 called the exception clause. Here's what it says. Matthew 19:9 says, "anyone who divorces his wife, except for marital unfaithfulness, and marries another woman commits adultery". And in Matthew 5:32 it says the same thing, "Anyone who divorces his wife, except for marital unfaithfulness, causes her to commit adultery".

Many scholars believe that Jesus is saying here that if adultery occurs in the marriage, God says it's okay to divorce and presumably remarry without incurring the sin of adultery. There's a few problems with that.

First, what about all the people in church who are divorced and remarried where adultery didn't happen in the first marriage? If that's what Jesus meant then we have two classes of second marriages. We have the better ones where adultery happened and remarriage is allowed, and the second class ones where adultery didn't happen.

A second problem is this. If adultery did happen, which partner can get remarried --- the innocent partner or both? If you say both, then the guy who committed adultery and remarries is in a legitimate second marriage while the guy who divorced where there was no adultery and remarries is in an illegitimate marriage. If you say only the innocent person is free to remarry, then what about the person who committed adultery in the first marriage and is now remarried and has a couple of kids and has now discovered Jesus and now reads the Bible and discovered that what he did was wrong? What's he supposed to do? Bottom line : if this is the case, then if you're going to divorce, then you might as well go out and make sure adultery is part of the equation.

There is a third problem with the traditional interpretation of Jesus' exception clause. It would neutralize what Jesus taught about divorce. We've just seen in Mark 10 that Jesus said divorce was man's plan. It shatters the divine plan. It shreds what God put together. And finally, divorce causes adultery. It doesn't make sense that Jesus would then say, but if adultery occurs in the marriage it's okay to divorce.

A fourth problem is that this would make adultery an unpardonable sin. Jesus, in Matthew 18, had given a powerful demonstration of the necessity for forgiveness, in response to Peter's question, "How many times must I forgive my brother?" Jesus answers, "Up to seventy times seven." In other words, infinity. Jesus makes this very clear by teaching the parable of the unmerciful servant, which strongly illustrates the critical importance of forgiving others, because God is a forgiving God. If adultery is a legitimate reason for divorce, then adultery falls outside the scope of a person's obligation to forgive.

So what could Jesus mean by this exception clause then? Here's what I believe is the best, and most consistent, interpretation of Jesus' words. Jesus uses two different words to describe sexual deviance in the passages dealing with the exception clause. The word that's used to describe sexual deviance in the first marriage is a different word from the word used to describe sexual deviance in the second marriage. The word "marital unfaithfulness", describing sexual deviance in the first marriage, is the Greek word "pornea." It's a broad term meaning a wide range of sexual deviance, even including prostitution. And the tense suggests that sexual deviance in the first marriage is likely going on for a prolonged period of time.

The word for adultery that's used to describe sexual deviance in the second marriage is a very narrow word that describes a sexual encounter with someone outside of the first marriage. And the tenses suggest that the adultery that takes place in a second marriage is a one-time event.

Here's the point. If sexual deviance occurs in the first marriage, adultery is not committed in the second marriage because the adultery has already happened in the first marriage. This isn't ground for divorce, it's simply a statement of fact. It would also seem to imply that if a person divorces where there is no adultery and remarries, and by way of consequence commits adultery, it's only adultery the first time. Jesus may even be inferring with the use of the two words for sexual deviance, that the primary problem is the sexual deviation in the first marriage since, in the context, that's the one that can be, and needs to be, redeemed.

Now, let's apply all this. What if you're single? You have a choice to make. You will either view marriage from the world's perspective or from God's perspective. The world's perspective is Kim Kardashian's perspective. Her marriage lasted 72 days. That's why young people shack up. They conclude, "Why bother getting married?" I do weddings where more come to the reception than the wedding ceremony. If you take God's perspective, then marital failure is not an option.

What if you're married and in a God blessed marriage? Be grateful. You've worked hard and God has honoured you.

What if you're married and miserable? Someone in the marriage has a hard heart. That's not what God intended. Surrender your marriage to God. Ask the Lord to soften hearts. And say, "Lord, I'm willing to do whatever it takes."

What if you're going through a divorce? Again, somebody had a hard heart. Surrender it to God. Is it your fault? Repent. Turn back. Discover God's blueprint. Be the husband God called you to be. A kind, respectful, humble, person of prayer. Is it the other person's fault? Maybe they committed adultery? It's not the unpardonable sin. Ask for God's grace to forgive. The most powerful legacy you can leave your children is magnanimous forgiveness in the face of great personal injury.

Remember Mark 10: 2? Jesus is answering the question, "Is it lawful for a man to divorce his wife?" Jesus' teaching is exclusively related to people who are currently married. He's not addressing divorced or remarried people. So His teaching applies to everybody I've described up to here. Don't divorce. For people who are already divorced you have to consult the rest of Scripture for direction.

What if you're divorced and single? Don't despair. Life is not over. Recognize that you sinned. You can't claim total innocence. If you haven't already done so, confess your sin. You were one half of a union that shattered the divine plan. That's worth weeping over. If you committed adultery you need to weep over that. But you need to own up, because if you minimize your responsibility for sin, you lose out on the wonder of God's amazing grace. 1 John 1:9 says, "If we confess our sins He is faithful and just to forgive us our sins and cleanse us from all unrighteousness." That includes divorce and adultery. Divorce is not unforgiveable. Adultery is not unforgiveable.

You have a number of things to consider. If you and your ex are still unmarried and still single, you need to explore the possibility of remarrying her or him. 1 Corinthians 7:10-11 say, "a wife is not to depart from her husband but if she does depart, let her remain unmarried or be reconciled to her husband. And a husband is not to divorce his wife." If your ex-partner is remarried, then remarriage is an option for you. 1 Corinthians 7:15 says, "if the unbeliever departs let him depart, a brother or sister is not under bondage in such cases." 1 Corinthians 7:27 says, "Are you loosed from a wife? Do not seek a wife. But if you do marry you have not sinned."

What if you're married again? Be grateful for the blessing of a second chance. Celebrate it. If you haven't already done so, confess your sin over the divorce. God is the God of the second chance. Jeremiah 18:1-6 says that God is the Potter who makes something new, out of something broken. He can exchange beauty for ashes.

Study Questions
1. What is your response to Jesus' description of marriage?

2. How do you respond to Jesus' teaching about divorce?

3. Compare the state of marriages in the New Testament with the state of marriages in our culture.

4. Respond to the interpretation of the "exception clause" discussed in the chapter.

5. How has this chapter changed your thinking about marriage and divorce?

CHAPTER 6

SEXUALITY:

GOD'S PLAN FOR A GREAT SEX LIFE

Let's talk about sex. Let's not talk about sex and the culture. We're all overdosed on sex in the media, movies, music industry, sports, advertising, and on the internet. Let's also not talk about sex and what I think. Who needs another opinion about sex? What I want to talk about here is God's Plan For A Great Sex Life. I think you're going to be surprised and interested and your thinking will be provoked by what God says in Scripture about sex. So let's jump right in.

First, sex was God's idea.

In my opinion, sex was one of God's most fantastic gifts. When it says in the Bible that God created Adam in His own image, that means humans were the magnum opus of His creative power. Psalm 139 says we were fearfully and wonderfully made. We are God's workmanship (Ephesians 2:10). You bear the fingerprint of God on your life. A few months ago I prayed for a couple of babies in our church. Here's what I prayed:

> "Father, Your Word says that you knit these little ones together in their mother's womb. They are fearfully and wonderfully made. They bear Your divine fingerprint on their lives. They were made in Your image. They are a special and unique creation, of a good and all powerful God. They are

not the product of evolutionary chance. They are the climax of Your creation, the magnum opus of the greatest artist in the universe. You masterminded the exact combination of DNA chromosomes that constituted their genetic code. You decided the colour of their hair, their eyes, their laugh, their gifts, their personality. You determined the exact time and circumstances of their birth You knew the exact number of hairs on their head. You knew them both even before they were conceived. They are as unique as every snowflake differs from the rest. They are Your treasured possession. You said that all of their days are written in Your Book. Your plan for them has always been filled with hope, love, joy and peace. You have loved them with an everlasting love. And we thank You for them. Amen."

That's the Bible's position on the value of human life. Pretty impressive, huh? And guess what? God created all of us as sexual beings, with the capacity for sexual experience. Sex was God's idea. Sex isn't dirty. It's not evil. It's not shameful. It's a fantastic gift of a good, gracious and creative God.

Back up a bit. Sex requires two people. God created us as relational people, with a longing for relationships. That's what God meant when He said, in Genesis 2, "It is not good for man to be alone". He's not just talking about marriage, He's talking about a need for friends. He was declaring that we all need friends. That's why friendship matters so much to us. That's why we hate loneliness. That's why photo albums and Facebook pictures usually have pictures of you and other people. God made us for relationship. He said, "Two are better than one, for when they lie down together, they keep each other warm." (Ecclesiastes 4:11) So God gave Eve to Adam to fulfill a deep relational need that all of us have experienced ever since. That's why God said, "A man will leave his father and mother and be joined to his wife and the two shall become one flesh." (Genesis 2:24) And God designed sexual intimacy to be the physical expression of that profound one-flesh union. Sex was God's idea. Here's the second thing God wants you to know about sex.

Second, sex is fun.

Sex was designed for three purposes: procreation, pleasure and the development of intimacy. God said to Adam and Eve, "Go forth and multiply." (Genesis 1:28) That's procreation, having kids. And that's the only commandment that mankind has faithfully obeyed since the Garden of Eden.

But pleasure was the second reason God created sex. You can see this quite clearly in the Song of Solomon. Some people won't read the Song of Solomon because they think it's 'R-rated'. It's a book about two lovers. The Beloved and her Lover, they're called. And some of the descriptions in this book are pretty hot. Steam room hot. Somebody asked me one time if the book was available on DVD. For example in Song of Solomon, chapter 5, she says to him, "My beloved is white and ruddy, chief among 10,000. His head is like the finest gold. His locks are wavy and black as a raven. His eyes are like doves by the rivers of waters, washed with milk and fitly set. His cheeks are like a bed of spices, banks of scented herbs. His lips are lilies, dripping liquid myrrh. His hands are rods of gold set with beryl. His body is carved ivory inlaid with sapphires" (v.5-14). Here's how to impress a guy. "His legs are pillars of marble set on bases of fine gold. His countenance is like Lebanon, excellent as the cedars. His mouth is most sweet. Yes, he is altogether lovely. This is my beloved. And this is my friend" (v.15-16). Hot stuff.

Then in chapter 6 the Lover writes a description of His beloved, and he says this, "O my love, you are as beautiful as Tirzah, lovely as Jerusalem. Awesome as an army with banners." (v.4) He really admires this woman. "Turn your eyes away from me, for they have overcome me." (v.5a) Her eyes must be really something. Maybe ice blue. For when he looks at her, his legs wobble. "Your hair is like a flock of goats going down from Gilead" (v.5b). Now, that's a cultural thing. She would have understood that as a beautiful compliment. It wasn't an insult. It means her hair was flowing. "Your teeth are like a flock of sheep which have come up from the washing, every one bears twins, and none is barren among them." (v.6) Her teeth are white and even, and there's none missing.

Then he goes on in chapter 7 and describes her from the feet up. Hang on to your seat. "How beautiful are your feet in sandals." (v.1a) He likes her feet especially when they're in sandals. He wouldn't have appreciated Uggs. "The curves of your thighs are like jewels. The work of the hands of a skillful workman." (v.1b) Wow. This is great stuff. "You are a fine piece of craftsmanship," he's saying. Now he's moving on up. "Your navel is a rounded goblet." He's at the bellybutton now. "It lacks no blended beverage." (v.2) Her bellybutton is deep. "Your waist is a heap of wheat set about with lilies." (v.2b) Ever see a bale of wheat sitting in a field, all tied up with a little narrow middle? He's saying she's shaped like an hour glass. See, how he moves from the feet, to the thighs, to her bellybutton? Now he moves on up, and says, "Your two...." hold on now, "Your two breasts are like two fawns, twins of a gazelle. Your neck is like an ivory tower. Your eyes like the pools in Heshbon." (v.3-4a) Looking into her eyes was like looking into pools of liquid. "Your nose is like the tower of Lebanon." (v.4b) That's another cultural thing. He's not talking smack about her nose here. This is a beautiful thing. "Your head crowns you like Mount Carmel, and the hair of your head is like purple. A king is held captive by your tresses. How fair and how pleasant you are, O love with your delights. This stature of yours is like a palm tree," (v.5-7a). He's saying, "this body of yours is like a palm tree." Now listen to this. "And your breasts like it's fruit. I said, 'I will go up to the palm tree and I will take hold of its fruit.'" (v.7b-8a)

God put all that in the Bible so that you would know that sex was for fun, for pleasure. Now, all that was foundational to what I want to say now. I want to walk you through 1 Corinthians 6 and 7, and show you the other principles God lays down for sex. Here's the third principle.

Third, sex was designed for marriage

1 Corinthians 7:1-2 says, "Now concerning the things of

which you wrote to me…". The context makes clear that the Corinthian Church is asking about sex. They have jotted down some questions for Paul and sent them to him. And now he's answering them. Here's what he says, "It is good for a man not to touch a woman." If you're single, that is; not if you're married. Because further on in the text, he says the exact opposite if you're married. If you're married, he says "don't stop touching her". But if you're not married, "it's good for a man not to touch a woman". It's good not to have sex. See, here's where Christ and culture collide. The culture says, "It's good for a young single person to have sex. In fact, if you haven't had sex by the time you're 15, there's probably something wrong with you." You may never hear someone bluntly say that, but so many young people secretly think that. God's plan for safe sex, is to save sex. Then Paul goes on, "Nevertheless, because of sexual immorality…". The culture of the day practiced causal sex: both fornication and adultery --- sex between singles and affairs with married people. Paul continues, "let each man have his own wife, and let each woman have her own husband". God put a fence around sex and called it marriage.

My dad built a fence around our garden when I was growing up as a wee boy in Belfast. He had the most beautiful roses in our neighbourhood. He had red roses, white roses, yellow roses and blue roses, and you could smell the fragrance of those roses from the bottom of our street. But rose gardens are delicate and fragile and easily damaged. They don't stand much chance of survival under the heavy trampling of a careless boot. So my dad built a fence all the way around his roses, to protect them and keep them safe from harm. Sexuality is like a rose garden. It's a beautiful thing. But it's delicate and fragile, easily damaged or destroyed if trampled carelessly. So God put this fence called marriage around your sexuality to keep it safe and protected, that it might always be a thing of beauty to be delighted in with your marriage partner for the rest of your lives.

Now, God knows that we are going to need more information about sex, if we're going to heed God's plan for a great sex life. So The Apostle Paul gives six reasons in chapter six why God put this fence around sex. Here they are.

First, sex is more than a physical act.

A lot of people wonder what the big deal is about sex, anyway. They say it's just a bodily function. Just a physical act. Actually, it's not just a physical act. Paul says, "Now the body is not for sexual immorality but for the Lord, and the Lord for the body" (1 Corinthians 6:13). Paul is saying God gave you your physical body so that you could honour God with it. Verse 20 says, "Glorify God in your body and in your spirit, which are God's." So when you have sex outside the perimeters God put around sex, you're doing something with your body that God hadn't intended.

Second, sexual intimacy for followers of Christ is a picture of their union with Christ.

Paul says, "Do you not know that your bodies are members of Christ? Shall I then take the members of Christ and make them members of a harlot?" (6:15). There was a practice at that time in the Roman Empire where they believed that sex was a way to get closer to the pagan gods. So they had prostitutes in the temple to help with acts of sexual worship. The Christians in the Church at Corinth coming out of that system liked that idea, especially the men, and so they were trying to introduce it in the church. And that's why Paul says what he says in this verse. He's saying, "Sex within the framework of marriage is a beautiful picture of your relationship with Christ and you're destroying that imagery." You're making it a mockery. Paul further describes how marriage is a picture of union with Christ in Ephesians 5.

He says a man loves his wife the way Christ loved the church. She respects him the way the church is to respect and honour Christ. They commit to each other for life the way Christ is committed to us eternally. And finally, a husband and wife commit to each other by faith and profound promise the way a Christian commits to Christ by faith.

That's why sex on the wedding night is so significant. Because it is the symbol of a commitment that has taken a long time in the making. The world's motivation for having sex is immediate pleasure. God's intention is that sex is a profound symbol of a permanent commitment. When I do weddings, in the middle of the ceremony after the couple has exchanged vows, I ask the young couple getting married, "Do you both promise that you will never seek to end this marriage in a court of law by divorce?"

If you are a committed follower of Jesus Christ, and you are a single person and are having sex with your partner, here's what Jesus Christ is calling you to do. Express a permanent, lifelong commitment of faith to each other, before God and in public. That's what we call a wedding. And that's what the sex act means.

Third, sex is a picture of the profound oneness in marriage. Paul says, "Or do you not know that he who is joined to a harlot (that's a euphemism for sexual intercourse) is one body with her? For the two shall become one flesh" (1 Corinthians 6:16). Sexual intimacy is the physical symbol of the mystical union that occurs between a man and a woman when they get married. To illustrate this with young people, I take a strip of duct tape, and lay it on some carpet. Then I pull it off the carpet and repeat the process a few times. Pretty soon the stickiness is gone. Sex was designed by God to be the physical bonding reflective of the spiritual bonding. When a person engages in sex with multiple partners, sexuality eventually loses its mystical bonding properties, like a piece of duct tape that has been repeatedly stuck and peeled off again.

Fourth, sexual sin has unique and deep consequences. Paul says, "Every sin that a man commits is outside the body, but he who commits sexual immorality, sins against his own body" (6:18). This is a difficult verse to fully understand. But it seems to be saying that there is something about sexual sin that causes damage that is more profound than any other sin. Imagine two pieces of cardboard glued together with strong adhesive. When the two pieces of cardboard are pulled apart, each sheet shreds part of the other and takes pieces with it. So it is with sex. Because sex is so profound and is not just a physical act, each person tears something profound from the other, and it is lost forever.

Fifth, God made sex to work best in the context of marriage. When you buy a new car, it's always best to follow the manufacturer's instructions if you want to take the best care of it. The instructions tell you when to change the oil, check the tire pressure, get a tune up, etc. When you do that, the car will work best and last a lot longer. God made you and He knows what works best Verse 19 says, "Do you not know that your body is the temple of the Holy Spirit who is in you, whom you have from God, and you are not your own? For you were bought at a price: therefore glorify God in your body, and in your spirit, which are God's." God owns you. He dwells inside you if you have committed your life to Him. He bought you at the price of the death of His Son Jesus Christ. And He designed you to enjoy sex. And He gave you a manual called the Bible, and told you how to protect your sexuality, and how to make it work best.

Sixth, sexual purity is redemptive. We have two choices in this matter of sexuality. We will either choose the path of the culture or the path of Christian character. You cannot do both, for they are mutually exclusive. They travel in opposite directions. They never meet; they collide. Consider the claims of the culture regarding sex :

Saving sex for marriage is quaint, old-fashioned, paternalistic and unrealistic. You should have sex whenever you want, with whomever you want, as often as you want, and if you're not, there may be something wrong with you. Be sure to be protected always, unless with a trusted friend, and in the event one of you make a mistake and get pregnant, either have the baby, get the baby adopted, or make an appointment with Planned Parenthood and they'll put you in touch with a reputable abortion doctor, in which case the baby is a fetus, a non-person. Unless of course, you change your mind about the abortion, in which case, the fetus will automatically become a baby again. Ironically, the abortion doctor is likely to have an office in the hospital next door to a surgeon who performs operations on pre-born babies and saves their lives in the womb. Finally, if you're sexually miserable , see a sex therapist: one who will advocate safe sex, and who will definitely never counsel you to save sex.

If you subscribe to this cultural philosophy of sex, let me ask you this: How's that working out for you? On the other hand, here's God's prescription for sex. "It is good for a man not to touch a woman" (1 Corinthians 7:1). It is a redemptive thing to protect and preserve this beautiful, fragile rose garden of your sexuality for marriage. God promises that He will bless you for your faithful commitment to do that. If you are already sexually active, you can still make a commitment today to stay sexually pure from now until your wedding day.

Fourth, God has a plan for a great sex life.

In the opening verses of 1 Corinthians chapter 7, the Apostle Paul describes six principles for a fulfilling sex life. First, is the principle of exclusivity. 7:2 says, "let each man have his own wife, and let each woman have her own husband". The principle of exclusivity says, "a married man should never have eyes for another woman, nor should a woman have eyes for another man". A partner should never seek sex with anyone outside of the marriage relationship.

Second, is the principle of mutual affection. 7:3 says, "Let the husband render to his wife the affection due her, and likewise also wife to her husband". Paul develops this further in Ephesians 5 when he says, "care for your wife the way you care for your own body". That means treating each other with tenderness, kindness, and sensitivity. The way you would care for your toe when you stub it on the bottom of the bed. The best way to stoke the fires of sexual intimacy is by demonstrating affection in word and deed, and lots of it, over a prolonged period of time. Someone said, "Sex begins in the kitchen." That means it begins at breakfast time, first thing in the morning, with affectionate words and touch, and carries on through the day until it climaxes in the bedroom at the end of the day. You can't starve the relationship of affection all day and expect a tiger in the bedroom at night.

By the way, mutual affection also includes an absence of harsh, rude, and unbecoming words and behaviour. A month of affection doesn't make up for a harsh word, or hostile action.

Third, is the principle of mutual selflessness. 7:4 says, "The wife does not have authority over her own body, but the husband does. And likewise, the husband does not have authority over his own body, but the wife does." When a couple get married, they say to each other, "What's mine is yours." Paul would say that's true, and it includes your body. That means each will selflessly serve the needs and desires of the other. It also means you won't use sex to control or manipulate, in order to get what you want. You won't withhold sex in order to punish the other. You won't demand sex. You won't make your partner do something they don't want to do, or aren't comfortable doing.

Sex is to be experienced in the context of love. I usually ask a couple who want to get married, "Do you love each other?" Then I quickly add, "Before you answer that question, let me read for you the Biblical definition of love first." Then I read 1 Corinthians 13. "Love is patient , love is kind. It does not envy. It is not proud. Love always protects… always hopes…etc." Then I add, "This is the brand of love that carries a marriage the distance. Now do you both love each other?" That's selflessness.

Fourth, is the principle of regularity. 7:5 says, "Do not deprive one another, except with consent for a time." That means have sex regularly. It's an important part of maintaining intimacy.

Fifth, is the principle of transparent communication. Notice again, 7:5 says, "Do not deprive one another, except with consent for a time." If you take a break make sure that it is by mutual agreement. That means you talk about it. Great sex is the result of clear understanding. The Apostle Peter says, "live with your wife with understanding" (1 Peter 3:7). That includes understanding sexual needs, desires, fears, concerns, etc.

Sixth, is the principle of spiritual vitality. Spiritual health is the pathway to sexual health. 7:5 says, "that you may give yourselves to prayer and fasting. And come together again, so that Satan does not tempt you because of your lack of self control." Satan attacks marriages by attacking the sexual health of the marriage. Many divorces are paved by sexual frustration.

Seventh, is the principle of enjoyment. 7:9 says, "if they cannot exercise self control let them marry, for it is better to marry than to burn with passion". Most of us have a natural sexual desire, that is satisfied in the context of loving, sexual intimacy. We started off this chapter by establishing that one of the purposes of sex was pleasure. And there's the pleasure right there. Sex was designed to be enjoyed. If it's causing frustration, or guilt, or tension, or anxiety, then it's not being practiced the way God intended it to be enjoyed.

Sexuality is a gift from God. But in our quest for pleasure, we often pervert God's gifts, and use them in ways they were never intended. God promises when you use His gifts according to the manufacturer's instructions, life works best. When we pervert their natural use, we settle for far less than God wants to give us.

C. S. Lewis said,

> "Indeed, if we consider the unblushing promises of reward and the staggering nature of the rewards promised in the Gospels, it would seem that Our Lord finds our desires, not too strong, but too weak. We are half-hearted creatures, fooling about with drink and sex and ambition when infinite joy is offered us, like an ignorant child who wants to go on making mud pies in a slum because he cannot imagine what is meant by the offer of a holiday at the sea. We are far too easily pleased."

Study Questions

1. What do you think of God's marriage "fence" around sexuality?

2. Which reasons for saving sex for marriage seem most meaningful to you?

3. What do you think of the principles for a great sex life found in 1 Corinthians 7?

4. Discuss the following statement: "Consider the claims of the culture regarding sex. 'Saving sex for marriage is quaint, old-fashioned, paternalistic and unrealistic. You should have sex whenever you want, with

whomever you want, as often as you want, and if you're not, there may be something wrong with you.'"

5. What surprised you most about this chapter?

CHAPTER 7

CRITICISM:

HOW TO KEEP THE HIPPOS OFF YOUR WINDPIPE

In my first year of ministry, I heard a pastor preach a message about how to stay alive in ministry. His title was "How to keep the elephants off your air hose". He said, "There's a lot of elephants out there, and if you let them step on your air hose, they'll cut off your oxygen and you'll suffocate." That was 25 years ago, and I've seen a lot of elephants and hippos since then. The Apostle Paul came across a lot of elephants that tried to step on his air hose, and in his first letter to the Corinthians chapter 4:1-5, Paul deals with the problem of criticism. I want to show you four words that Paul used to handle the problem of criticism and which kept the hippos off his windpipe. Because you don't just want to survive in ministry, you want to thrive. Here's the first word.

Be Faithful.

That's two words actually. Here's what he says, in verse 2, "It is required in a steward that he be found faithful." I've done a lot of weddings over the years, and I've never yet seen an ugly bride. One time a minister was standing at the front of the church along with the groom and his best man, and this beautiful bride was coming down the aisle, and the groom whispered, "She looks like a goddess", to which his best man said, "Take a good look, she'll never look this good again." That's a terrible thing to say. That's not true. So many things start out so well, like marriages and ministry, yet so many end so poorly. It's easy to start well. It's another thing entirely to finish well.   And the key to a successful marriage and a successful ministry is faithfulness.   Faithfulness is a commitment to keep your promises, even when the conditions under which the original promise was made change.

Notice, Paul doesn't say, "It is required in a steward that he be found to have a big church, or earn a huge paycheque, or earn a pile of degrees with more letters behind the name than the post office has."   It's required that he be found faithful. At the finish line I won't be assessed by the size of my church, or the number of conversions, or number of baptisms, or the size of the church budget, or the oratory excellence of my sermons; I'll be assessed by my faithfulness. The world, and unfortunately sometimes the Christian community, measure by outward appearances; God measures the heart. God told Samuel, when David was being tapped for the role of the King, "Man looks at the outward appearance, but the Lord God looks at the heart" (1 Samuel 16:7). We measure with a yard stick, God measures with a dip stick.

Our youngest daughter is 18 now, and she announced a while ago that it was time for her to get her driving licence. I didn't sleep very well for a few nights after that announcement, because I knew it would be me who would get the job of teaching her how to drive. Because her mother has a rule : she refuses to drive with anyone who does not know how to drive. So we started the lessons, and I said to her, "Being a good driver is a matter of learning a whole bunch of little habits, like always remembering where the brake pedal is, and always stopping when the light is red. That's really important." She took this one so seriously that when the light turned green she kept asking: "Is it okay for me to go now?" Good driving is doing a whole bunch of little things well. Always checking over your shoulder, and always checking your blind spot, and always checking your mirrors. Always driving in your lane, and always using your signal, and always driving below the speed limit. On that one she asked, "Then how come you don't." Smart kid. Too smart sometimes. So long as you faithfully remember to do all these little things well, you'll be a good driver. And she's faithfully practicing all these little habits and she's doing really well now. Almost to the point where her mother is willing to drive with her.

Faithfulness in ministry is like being a good driver. It's a matter of doing a whole bunch of little things well, every day. It's a matter of faithfully praying every day, reading the word every day, making wise decisions every day, doing your best every day. Doing more than is asked or required of you. Fulfilling your responsibilities every day. Connecting with lost people every day. Connecting with the people you lead every day. Keeping your word every day. Saying no to impure choices every day. Faithfulness is keeping your promises even when the circumstances change under which the original promise was made. That's how marriages and ministries last a lifetime.

C.H. Spurgeon said, "I'd rather be a fool and do what Christ tells me, than be the wisest man of the modern school, and despise the Word of the Lord." Be faithful.

Here's the second word, or two words.

Be Tough.

I saw a bumper sticker a while ago. It said "When the going gets tough, the tough go golfing." Paul would say "When the going gets tough, plough on." Verse 3 says, "It is a very small thing that I should be judged by you." He's being criticized. Talked about. Slandered, even. The going is getting tough. Ever notice a flock of Canada geese flying in that V-formation? The goose at the apex of the "v" can only lead for a while, then he drops back and another fella takes over. You know why? Because the fella at the front takes the bulk of the wind resistance. You can't lead without encountering resistance. In fact, if there's no resistance, you're probably not leading.

My first car when I was 17, growing up in Belfast, was a Mini Minor. What a bucket of bolts that was. My friends called it a Rolls Cinardly. Because they said, "It rolls down the hill and can 'ardly get up again." The tires were balder than me. And I got so many punctures in the tires of that car, I was fixing flat tires every weekend. Criticism is like a slow leak puncture hole in your tire. It doesn't stop you right away, but it can slowly deflate you. To change the metaphor, criticism can take the wind out of your sails. It can suck the oxygen out of your lungs. I would estimate that one critical word can eclipse 10 words of encouragement. Put another way, it takes about ten words of encouragement to replenish the emotional drain of one harsh, critical statement. I can't back up those figures from Scripture. But trust me, it's true. I speak from experience.

Notice what Paul says in verse 3. "But with me it is a very small thing that I should be judged by you, or by any human court." In other words, Be tough. Don't let criticism get you down. It's a small thing. You may be thinking, "Paul, you don't know how hurtful it is to be criticized. It's easy for you to say it's just a small thing." But it is such a small thing. Compared with a child on the cancer ward at Toronto Sick Kids Hospital, dealing with leukemia, criticism is a small thing.

When you experience criticism, be tough. Now, this doesn't mean you don't listen to criticism. Just don't listen to useless criticism. Don't listen to criticism from just anybody. What you want to do is create redemptive, intentional criticism. Assemble your own critical team. Surround yourself with a team of wise, mature, trusted, thoughtful men and women. Be accountable to them. Let them speak truth into your life, and let them teach you.

Theodore Roosevelt wrote these wise words.

"It is not the critic who counts; not the man who points out how the strong man stumbles or where the doer of deeds could have done them better.

The credit belongs to the man who is actually in the arena, whose face is marred by dust and sweat and blood, who comes short, for there is no effort without error. Far better it is to dare mighty things, to win glorious triumphs, even though checkered by failure, than to take rank with those poor souls who neither enjoy much nor suffer much, because they live in the gray twilight that knows neither victory nor defeat."

Be faithful and be tough.

The third set of words Paul would tell us is : Be Humble.

Paul goes on, "I know of nothing against myself, yet I am not justified by this." Notice what he's saying here: "I think my motives are pure, but I can't be sure." Humility is the recognition that even when I think I'm right, I know that I might be wrong. When I think my motives are pure, I admit that they may be tainted. Humility is the antibiotic that kills the infection of pride.

Humility is the ability to recognize that God can turn bleak situations in my life into redemptive outcomes. My dad grew the most beautiful roses in our neighbourhood back in Belfast. You could smell his roses from the bottom of the street. And a couple of times a year this old fella would come around our door with a horse and cart collecting old clothes. And the horse would do its business right outside our door. It was like he was doing my dad a favour, because my dad would shovel it up and throw it round the roses. I could never understand how my dad could grow such beautiful roses out of something so putrid as horse manure. And yet that's what God does. Out of the soil of Good Friday, God grew the beauty of Easter Sunday. Out of the soil of betrayal, Joseph said to his brothers, "What you meant for evil God meant for good" (Gen.50:20). God can take the bleakest of life's circumstances and grow the most beautiful roses, so long as you respond to the soil of adversity with a spirit of humility.

Humility is the realization that anything good in me comes from God, and that God has undeservedly blessed us beyond measure, and that with great privilege comes great responsibility. It's the realization that you deserved hell and got heaven. It's the realization that you didn't get where you are by yourself. God put you there. 1 Corinthians 12:18 says, "He places each one in the Body as He pleases." And He can take us out in an instant. Job declared, "The Lord giveth and the Lord taketh away; blessed be the name of the Lord." (Job 1:21) So we take our position, and all that we possess, and all that we enjoy and we hold it very loosely in an open hand, not in a closed fist. That's the essence of humility.

Then here's the last two words. Be Focused.

Verse 4 says, "He who judges me is the Lord......Each one's praise will come from God." Paul is focused on the applause of heaven. If you ever ran track you know the power of the grandstand. When we were kids we ran track at school, and all the parents and grandparents would be up in the grandstand. And we would run the first, second, and third bends without spectators. But as we would come round that last bend into the home stretch, the cheering and hollering from the grandstand was so loud and so powerfull that it set off the adrenal glands, and we would run faster and I would look up into the stands for the face of my grandfather, to see his smile, even though I was in the back of the pack. It's amazing, the power of the grandstand. As we track through life, many of us still run for the applause of the grandstand. Some of us are running to please a father or mother, or a wife or husband. Some pastors run to hear the applause, and feel the pleasure, of the congregation. And the problem with that is this : what happens when the applause stops?

What we need to do, is clear out the grandstand, and run the race for an Audience of One. And when the race is done, and you've fought the good fight, and kept the faith and finished the race, with faithfulness and with no regrets, you'll hear a roar, and it'll be the approval of heaven, and the applause of Christ, and He won't be in the grandstand --- He will be standing at the finish line and He'll wrap His arms around you, and He'll say, "Well done, my good and faithful servant."

There's an old hymn that starts like this.

"Oft times the day seems long, and sorrows hard to bear.

We're tempted to complain and murmur and despair,

But Christ will soon appear and catch His Bride away,

All tears will soon be over in God's eternal day."

And then the chorus

"It will be worth it all

When we see Jesus,

Life's trials will seem so small when we see Christ.

One glimpse of His dear face, all sorrow will erase,

So bravely run the race, till we see Christ."

Study questions

1. Can you think of a time when you were criticized and how it felt?

2. Why do you think criticism is sometimes so hard to accept?

3. Which of the four principles for combating criticism do you find most helpful, or most difficult to practice?

4. Discuss the following statement: "Criticism can take the wind out of your sails. It can suck the oxygen out of your lungs. I would estimate that one critical word can eclipse 10 words of encouragement."

5. What difference do you think it can make when we run for an Audience of One?

CHAPTER 8

PRAYER:

HOW DO I KNOW WHAT TO SAY?

Bill Hybels underscored the importance of prayer when he wrote a book entitled, "Too Busy Not To Pray". Someone once noted the consequences of not praying with this observation, "You can't force God to do anything He doesn't want to do. But you can prevent Him from doing what He does want to do." In other words, there are some things God wants to do in your life, and in your orbit, that He will do only if you pray.

But important as prayer is, most of us find prayer to be a challenge. Some people say they're too busy to pray, and can't find the time. Others say there are too many distractions in their life to pray. Still others say they don't know what to say when they pray. In Matthew 6:5-15, Jesus lays out a series of prayer principles that we will find helpful in developing a meaningful prayer life.

The Command to Pray

Jesus says in v.5, "And when you pray...". Notice Jesus doesn't say, "if you pray". He says "when", because He is assuming that prayer will be a reality in the life of His followers. Prayer is a command, and a responsibility, for a follower of Jesus. It's not optional. To not pray is sin. Samuel said, "Far be it from me that I should sin against the Lord in ceasing to pray for you" (1 Samuel 12:23). If we are in a relationship with God, that relationship will be dependent on communication. God is responsible for the breadth of our ministry. But we are responsible for the depth of our relationship with Him.

The Motive for Prayer

Jesus then cautions about praying with wrong motives. He says, "when you pray, you shall not be like the hypocrites…" (v.5). He's talking about the religious leaders who used prayer as an opportunity to show off. He says, "They love to pray… to be seen by men" (v.5). Their prayers were fake. The proper motive for prayer is to pray with a sincere heart, and a desire to communicate with the Lord. When praying in a group, it's important to not be too concerned about what others will think of your prayer, because you're praying for God's ears, and no one else's. Prayer is an expression of communication. Every relationship is built on communication. Real, authentic communication. Can you imagine how phony a relationship would be, if the communication was fake? Prayer with God should be real, and spontaneous, like a conversation between two people in love with one another.

The Plan for Prayer

While prayer is often spontaneous, for prayer to be a significant element of your life it should also be intentional and planned. Jesus was speaking about this planned prayer when He said, "when you pray, go into your room…and shut the door…" (v.6a). There are two principles involved in a planned prayer time. First, we need to find a private place to pray. That's the idea behind Jesus' words to "go into your room and shut the door". That's where you find privacy and freedom from distraction.

Then, second, you need to find a time in your day to go into this private place to pray, either early in the morning, or perhaps midday, after work, or last thing at night. Usually, whatever works best for you is best. Some of us are morning persons, others are night-hawks. Jesus prayed at all times of the day, sometimes early morning, sometimes at night, sometimes all night. David, in the Psalms, said, "Early will I seek Thee" (63:1). When you establish a time and a place to pray, the likelihood of establishing a consistent prayer time will dramatically increase. The time you spend in this planned prayer time is up to you. Look at this time like a spiritual gas station, which you pull into once a day to fill up your spiritual gas tank. If this time is new to you, then start with what you can manage. Better to start small and build up some successes, rather than to bite off more than you can chew, and get discouraged and quit. Consider Jesus' words as a goal to work towards, when the disciples slept while He prayed: "Could you not watch with me one hour?" (Matthew 26:40).

Obviously, Jesus is not restricting prayer to this private, closed door type of prayer. Prayer should also be practiced throughout the day. Paul said, "Pray without ceasing." (1 Thessalonians 5:17). Jesus' presence is with you 24/7. You can talk to Him anytime, in the car, on the subway, in the classroom, or at your desk. But all this prayer should be built on the foundation of an extended, uninterrupted, scheduled time for prayer.

The Focus of Prayer

Jesus then talks about the focus of our prayers. He says, "pray to your Father..." (v.6b, 8). See the intimacy of this relationship. Nowhere in the Old Testament is God referred to as "Father." It's Jesus who reveals this quality of the Fatherhood of God. Jesus goes so far as to call Him "Abba," which is an even more affectionate term, meaning "daddy." Notice He says, "your Father". He is our personal Father. He knows us intimately. He has the characteristics of any wise, loving, protective, gracious human father --- to perfection. Jesus said, "If you then, being evil, know how to give good gifts to your children, how much more will your Father who is in heaven, give good things to those who ask Him" (Matthew 7:11). That's the manner in which we should approach God in prayer, as our Father. We can talk to Him about anything that is on our heart, just the way a child can approach a wise, good and gracious earthly father.

The Expectation of Prayer

Because we are praying to our Father, we should approach Him with expectant hearts. Jesus says, "And your Heavenly Father... will reward you openly" (v.6c). Our Father hears our prayers, because He cares about us. David says, in Psalm 40:1, "I waited patiently for the Lord, and He turned to me, and heard my cry." Notice God turns, then hears the cry. He turned before the cry was even uttered, because He knew it was coming. We can pray expectantly, because we know that God hears our prayers, and that He will reward our faithfulness. That doesn't necessarily mean that He will always give us what we pray for, but He will reward our faithfulness, which is enough of a promise to warrant our expectation. In other words, when God says He will reward, it doesn't really matter what form the reward takes, so long as it's a reward from the Father.

The Thoughtfulness of Prayer

Because we are praying to the Father, the communication should be as meaningful as that of a child talking with his earthly father. A child wouldn't speak to his father in a stain glass voice, from a memorized, formulaic script. And neither should we. Jesus says, "when you pray, do not use vain repetitions..." (v.7). Prayer should be a thoughtful, meaningful conversation. Merely reciting the same mantra, like a rosary, or even a thoughtless rendition of the Lord's prayer, would be an example of the vain repetition Jesus is talking about. Some traditions even use the Lord's prayer as a form of penance, by asking penitent sinners to recite the Lord's prayer multiple times, and the worse the sin, the more the recitations. Prayer is never to be vain repetition.

The Model For Prayer

Jesus recognizes the challenge of knowing what to say when we pray. In fact, the disciples on one occasion asked Jesus to teach them to pray. It seems that most of us struggle with this matter of knowing just how to pray. So Jesus continues with an example of how to pray. He says, "In this manner, therefore, pray..." (v.9-14). Then He provides this beautiful model for prayer, that is known the world over as The Lord's Prayer. It's actually more accurate to call it The Disciples' Prayer, because Jesus gave it as an example for us. The real Lord's Prayer is the one that's recorded in John 17.

The Disciples' Prayer was never intended to be recited verbatim, and certainly not multiple times. Its purpose was to show the various themes that prayer should include. In this model for prayer, we will see six themes that prayer should include.

1. Worship

The first theme in the prayer focuses on the Father, and His holiness: "Our Father in heaven, hallowed be Your Name..." (v.9b). So the first theme in our prayer should be concerned with worship, and adoration. It's helpful at this point to read some of the worship Psalms in a spirit of prayer, such as Ps.95, 96, 98, or 100. Another helpful way to worship is to sing worship and praise songs, or to read worship hymns from a hymn book. The idea here is to tell God how much you love Him, and to focus on His Character and His Works.

2. Surrender

Prayer is really about us lining up our heart with God's agenda. It's not primarily about me telling God what I want, it's about finding out what God wants to do in and through me. C.S. Lewis said, "Prayer does not so much change things, as it changes me." The next part of this prayer says, "Your

Kingdom come. Your will be done on earth as it is in heaven." God's will is done perfectly in heaven, and so Jesus is calling us to pray for God's will to be done perfectly also on earth. Prayer is a matter of bending and surrendering our agendas, desires, and ambitions to His program and plan for us. Jesus said it this way in the Garden of Gethsemane, "Not my will, but Thine be done" (Mark 14:36). So, in this prayer movement, you want to do a heart check, and freshly surrender your life and plans to Him, including your marriage, your job, your finances, your attitudes, kids, words, and relationships.

3. Requests

This is the prayer theme we are most familiar with --- making requests. Jesus said in the next theme in the prayer, "Give us this day our daily bread" (v.11). Bread is the basic sustenance of life. Prisoners used to survive on nothing more than bread and water. Jesus is teaching us to depend on God for the most basic necessities of life, including bread. This should cause us to realize that there is no request that is too small to bring to God. He cares about every concern on your heart. Nothing is too trivial for Him. Peter said, "Cast all your care on Him, because He cares for you" (1 Peter 5:7). This prayer focus will also produce a spirit of dependence. If we depend on Him for bread, we will depend on Him for everything. It also produces a spirit of gratitude. We recognize that even the loaf of bread on our table comes from God's gracious Hand. The job we have that allows us to make money comes from His Hand. The health we enjoy that enables us to work is because of His protective Hand. So, make requests. It's helpful to keep a list of requests, so that you will remember to pray for things that are important, especially when others ask you to pray. Without a list you may forget. The list also helps you to more readily identify answers to prayer.

4. Confession

Jesus goes on to say, "forgive us our debts". That means personal confession. David said in Psalm 139:23, "Search me, O God, and know my heart." That is a recognition that there might be wrongdoing in our lives of which we're not even aware. This is a good time to reflect on the past 24-hour period and consider whether you have spoken any offensive words, considered any offensive thoughts, harboured any offensive attitudes, committed any offensive behaviour, or failed to do something you should have done. The Bible says that God takes our sins and drops them into the deepest part of the ocean. That means He puts them in a place no man can get at. He's painting a picture that His forgiveness of our sin is so complete that once we confess it, it is banished forever, never to be brought up in accusation against us ever again.

5. Forgiveness

Prayer is more about changing us than it is about changing things. And Jesus now moves into the area of relational forgiveness, when He says, "as we forgive our debtors" (v.12b). Hurt people hurt other people, who then become angry. And anger over time produces bitterness. And bitterness produces hardening of attitudes. And that produces spiritual stagnation. Forgiveness allows you to become better rather than bitter. Prayer is the place to bring anyone in your life who has hurt you, or disappointed you, before the throne of grace; and just as you received God's love, grace and forgiveness, God enables you to extend the same to them. That's what Paul means when he writes, "And be kind to one another, tender-hearted, forgiving one another, even as God in Christ forgave you" (Ephesians. 4:32).

6. Purity

Jesus says, "And do not lead us into temptation" (v.13a). This does not mean that God would ever lead us into temptation.

James 1:13 says, "Let no one says when he is tempted, 'I am tempted by God,' for God cannot be tempted by evil, nor does He Himself tempt anyone." Jesus is telling us to ask the Father to keep us far away from tempting situations that can influence us towards impurity. He carries the same thought on in the next statement when he says, "But deliver us from the evil one" (v.13).

7. Praise

The final level of prayer in the Disciples' Prayer is praise. "For Yours is the kingdom, the power and the glory forever, amen." That's a fitting way to end prayer. Prayer begins with a focus on God and His character, and ends the same way.

The Power of Prayer

Jesus finishes this model prayer with these words, "If you forgive men their trespasses, your heavenly Father will also forgive you. But if you do not forgive men their trespasses, neither will your Father forgive your trespasses" (v.14-15). Clearly, these words are attached to the subject of prayer, because they pick up the same theme about forgiveness that was discussed in the prayer. Jesus is saying that when you have been forgiven, you will be so grateful that you will naturally forgive others. If you do not forgive others, then that's a sign that you have not really understood, or embraced God's grace and forgiveness towards you. So the marvellous power of prayer then, is that prayer enables you to experience God's forgiveness, and empowers you to extend that forgiveness and grace to others. Prayer is a key ingredient to forgiveness and relational harmony. Prayer is the oil that lubricates the gears of relationships.

Study Questions

   1. What do you find most challenging about prayer?

2. What was most helpful to you in the chapter on prayer?

3. Describe when and where you pray on a regular basis.

4. How do you respond to the pattern for prayer used in the Lord's prayer?

5. Respond to the following statement: "If you do not forgive others, then that's a sign that you have not really understood, or embraced, God's grace and forgiveness towards you. So the marvelous power of prayer then, is that prayer enables you to experience God's forgiveness, and empowers you to extend that forgiveness and grace to others."

CHAPTER 9

SUFFERING:

HOW CAN GOD BE GOOD, GREAT AND STILL ALLOW GRIEF?

The Bible doesn't sugarcoat suffering. In John 16:33, Jesus said, "In this life there will be trouble". James says, "When you fall into various trials" (James 1:2). Notice James doesn't say "if", but "when". Trouble is a certainty --- a fact of life. That word "fall" means "to stumble unexpectedly". Suffering comes without warning. The word "various" means that suffering comes in many different shades --- as many shades as the paint chips at a Benjamin Moore paint store. Suffering comes in various shades --- illness, injury, betrayal by a friend, loss, even violence, rape, murder. And all this causes people to ask, "If God is good, and God is great, why does He allow suffering?" Put another way, "if He cares, and if He can, why doesn't He step in and stomp it out? Why doesn't he show up and show off?" And some people have trouble believing in the God of the Bible because of the problem of suffering.

I should add at this point that the problem of suffering is not limited to Christianity. Every world faith has to answer the same question. When the Indonesian Tsunami hit the beaches in 2005, every faith had to wrestle with the reality of God and the existence of suffering. Some just couldn't accept that a good and powerful God could allow suffering of that magnitude. The Archbishop of Canterbury said, "This has made me question God's existence." Others just accepted it as an unexplainable mystery. Derrick Kidman, a British evangelical, said, "God is not accountable, and we can just never know the reasons why." Others believe that God is just not powerful enough to control catastrophes like the tsunami. Rabbi Michael Learner said, "God is simply not omnipotent. He's not powerful enough to stop a tsunami." Others believe suffering is God's judgment. A Saudi Cleric said about the tsunami, "The water rose to strike non-Muslim vacationers who lay sprawled immorally on the beach during Christmas break." In Sri Lanka, a Buddhist monk said, "The people are not living according to religious virtue. Nature is giving a punishment because people are not following the path of Lord Buddha." A Roman Catholic priest said the tsunami was a "punishment from God because everybody is living a wretched life". A fisherman in one of the worst hit villages said, "The mother has butchered her own children. Either there is no god or god must be cruel to do something like this."

Rabbi Harold Kushner wrote a book in the 1980's entitled *"Why Do Bad Things Happen To Good People?"* and asked this question: "How can God be a good and loving God, and also be a God who is all powerful and yet allow suffering, especially on such a cosmic scale?" He goes on to suggest that one of three things must be true: He is a loving God who would love to prevent tsunamis and suffering, but can't, because He is not powerful. Or He is powerful and could prevent tsunamis if He wanted to , but He didn't, because He's a cruel, malevolent God who doesn't care. Or maybe He is neither good nor powerful, because he exists only in the figment of our imagination. Kushner's conclusion was that God is a good God. But He's not omnipotent. He's not all-powerful. He would love to help, but He can't.

Warren Weirsbe wrote a rebuttal to Kushner's book, entitled, *"Why Do Bad Things Happen To God's People?"* and for his answers he turned to the Bible. That's what we want to do here. So let's get back to the Bible and get God's perspective on suffering.

The Reality of Suffering,

The Hindu faith teaches that suffering is an illusion. But the Bible clearly acknowledges the reality of suffering. In 2 Corinthians 12:7, we see an example of suffering in the life of the Apostle Paul. He writes, "A thorn in the flesh was given to me." Let's stop there for a moment. "A thorn in the flesh". We're familiar with that idiom. It's a common expression in the English language. If you have ever pruned roses, you know the pain of a misplaced thumb over the thorn of a rose bush, or the pain of a thorn that has gotten down into your shoe and under your foot. If someone is a real annoyance to you, or causes you a lot of grief, they are "a thorn in the flesh". Like a thorn in your shoe. So Paul has an assailant causing him a lot of grief, a lot of suffering. The text says it buffeted him. That's the reality of suffering. Paul suffered. We all experience suffering. Job says, "man is born to trouble as surely as the sparks fly upward" (Job 5:7). In 2 Corinthians 11:24-27, Paul lists all the ways in which he suffered. James said, "When you face troubles of many kinds" (James 1:2)

The Perplexity of Suffering

Paul pleaded with God to get rid of the suffering. Three times he prayed that God would take it from him (2 Corinthians 12:8). That's understandable. We hate suffering. We want rid of it. Habakkuk 1:2-3 say, "How long shall I cry and you will not hear? .... Why do you show me iniquity and cause me to see trouble?" The Bible never teaches that suffering should be glorified, or sought after. Job said throughout the first 37 chapters of the book, in so many words, "Lord, why is this happening to me?" Even the Lord Jesus, in the Garden of Gethsemane, said, "Father, if it is possible take this cup from me" (Matthew 26:39). Charles Templeton, a contemporary of Billy Graham, and fellow evangelist, who was drawing thousands to his crusades, lost his faith because of human suffering. When he looked at the picture of a starving little girl in a country torn by famine, he couldn't reconcile a good and powerful God with the stark reality of human suffering. Paul said, in 1 Corinthians 13:12, "For now we see in a glass darkly". In other words, there is much that we don't understand. Some years ago someone took a survey and asked the question, "If there was one question you could ask God, what would it be?" And the number one answer was, "Why is there suffering in the world?" Suffering is very perplexing.

The Origins of Suffering

There are three answers to the question about the origins, or causes, of suffering. First, Satan is the prime cause of much suffering. There's been a lot of speculation about the nature of Paul's thorn in the flesh. Some say it was a physical affliction, maybe blindness. Or perhaps a leftover physical injury type damage from the time he was stoned. But the text says it was a messenger from Satan. That word "messenger" is the word "angelos" meaning "angel". A satanic angel is a demon. I believe the thorn in the flesh was a demonic spirit that dogged Paul and caused him a lot of grief. The extreme example of this kind of suffering is seen in people who are demon-possessed. Note how many people Jesus encountered, who suffered because of satanic possession. Many of them were basically sociopaths, and caused much damage to themselves and other people. Psychopathic and sociopathic killers in our society are possessed by the same evil presence Jesus encountered in the Gospels.

The second cause of suffering is moral corruption. Some people say, "Why didn't God just make a world without pain and suffering and evil and death?" The answer is that He did. Genesis 1:31 says, "God saw all that He had made and it was very good." Some people say, "Then why didn't He just make Adam and Eve incapable of sin?" He didn't do that because He wanted people to love, and you can't love without choice. If you pull the string on a Barbie doll and it says, "I love you", you wouldn't get terribly excited about that, because it's just a doll and it's programmed to say that. It doesn't have any choice. You can't create the potential to love without also creating the potential for the flip side --- namely evil and wickedness. God said to Adam, "Don't eat of the tree of the knowledge of good and evil, for in the day you disobey me and eat it you will die." (Genesis 2:17) Two things happened when Adam disobeyed. First, he became intimately acquainted with evil. Notice, it was the tree of the Knowledge of Evil. He didn't know what evil was until that point, and from that moment on, evil began to pollute the universe. Romans 1:30 says that man will invent ways to do evil. And we see that happening in our day. Sin has marred our moral judgment, and causes us to intentionally and unintentionally create dangerous scenarios that result in pain, suffering and heartache. The second thing that happened was that death entered the world as a result of moral impurity. So much suffering is caused by the moral pollution in the world.

The third cause of suffering is natural corruption. Genesis 3:18 says that because sin entered the world, "thorns and thistles grew". The creation was tainted when moral corruption spilled into the cosmos. Romans 8:22 says, "all creation groans with pain like the pain of childbirth". The world, because of moral corruption, became a dangerous place. Natural corruption is the cause of earthquakes, tornadoes and underwater earthquakes that produce tsunamis which all cause unspeakable suffering. God never created evil and pain and death. It was humanity exercising self-centred free will that opened the door for human suffering. Larry King asked Anne Graham, after Hurricane Katrina, why a good God would allow such suffering, and Graham said, "Larry, for years this nation has been telling God to leave them alone, and God being the Gentleman that He is, honoured that request."

The Redemptive Value Of Suffering

God uses suffering to advance His redemptive and good purposes in your life. God never wastes a hurt. Romans 8:28 says, "For we know that all things (including pain and suffering) work together for good to those who love God." All suffering can produce God's benevolent and good purposes. There are four purposes for suffering revealed in the text here in 2 Corinthians 12.

The first is that suffering shapes character. Verse 7 says, "and lest I should be exalted above measure by the abundance of the revelations...". Paul has been talking about being taken up to the third heaven and receiving visions and revelations. What an experience that must have been. That kind of thing could go to a guy's head. Make him proud. But he says, "lest I should be exalted above measure... a thorn in the flesh was given to me". Suffering taught him humility. Romans 5:3 says, "We rejoice in our suffering because we know that suffering produces perseverance, perseverance character, and character, hope." Romans 8:29 says, "We have been called according to his purpose to be conformed to the character of Jesus Christ." One of the core characteristics of the character of Jesus is His prayer life. And suffering is part of God's curriculum to produce His character in our lives. Notice Paul prays three times for the suffering to end, and God says "No." Nowhere in the Bible does God use the term "unanswered prayer". What we often mean by unanswered prayer is that our prayers are not answered in a way that we expect, or even demand, God to answer them. Suffering has a way of producing an attitude adjustment, and conforming us to the character of Jesus Christ. Sometimes that suffering is discipline. Hebrews 12:10-11 says, "Our fathers disciplined us for a little while as they thought best. But God disciplines us for our good that we may share in His holiness. No discipline seems pleasant at the time, but painful. Later on however, it produces a harvest of righteousness and peace for those who have been trained by it."

The second purpose of suffering is that suffering produces a deeper level of intimacy with God. In verse 8, Paul goes on to say, "I pleaded with the Lord three times that it might depart from me". Paul's suffering has the result of drawing him closer to the Lord through prayer, as a direct result of his suffering. Paul said in Philippians 3:10, "I want to know Christ and the power of His resurrection...". That's understandable. That's what we all want. But he goes on in that verse to say, "and the fellowship of His suffering". He knows that the pathway to knowing Christ runs straight through the valley of suffering. When he suffers for Christ, he experiences the fellowship of Christ at an entirely new level. That's what King David meant when he said, "Yea, though I walk through the valley of the shadow of death, I will fear no evil, for you are with me...." (Psalm 23:4).

C.S. Lewis said, "God whispers to us in our pleasures. He speaks to us in our conscience. But He shouts to us in our pain. Pain is God's megaphone to arouse a deaf world." God speaks most clearly in the context of our pain. Many people have bowed the knee in surrender to Jesus Christ, because of the redemptive crucible of suffering. God used the suffering of a young 16-year-old by the name of Joni Erickson, when she dived off a rock, broke her neck on the lake bed and became a quadriplegic, to bring her to faith in Jesus Christ. Joni Erickson said, "I would rather be in this wheelchair in the will of God, than out of this chair, out of the will of God."

Through the Book of Job, we read of Job saying over and over, "Why is this happening to me?" Then at the end of the book, God showed up and He never answered Job's questions. God just said, "Where were you when I laid the foundations of the world?" (Job 38:4) In other words, "Who do you think you are, questioning me? I'm God, and you're not." And Job said, "My ears had heard of you. Now my eyes have seen you." (Job 42:5) Once Job heard God speak, he didn't need his questions answered. God's presence was enough. Suffering moved Job to a new dimension of intimacy with God. What we need in our suffering is not answers, as much as we need assurance of the reality of the Presence of God. David would say the same about suffering's redemptive power. In Psalm 119:67, David said, "Before I was afflicted I went astray but now I keep Your Word." He goes on in verse 71, to say, "It is good that I have been afflicted that I may learn your statutes."

The third purpose of suffering is that suffering exposes you to greater abundance of God's Grace. In verse nine, God responds to Paul's prayer by saying, "My grace is sufficient for you". When we suffer, God supplies His grace to meet the need. The greater the suffering the greater the supply of grace. The Bible says in James 4:6, "He gives more grace". There are two ways to respond to suffering, pain, injury and disappointment. The first alternative is to turn away from God and resist His grace and become hard, bitter, angry, cynical and disillusioned. That is a lonely, miserable road. The alternative is to turn toward God and open yourself to His grace. Grace is a gift and when you receive that gift you become more gentle, gracious, loving, tender, hopeful, kind, compassionate and grateful. Detrich Bonhoffer was a German follower of Christ, thrown into prison during the Second World War for his faith and outspoken views against the Nazi Regime, and God used prison in his life so powerfully, that he said, "Thank you prison for having been in my life."

The fourth purpose of suffering is that suffering showcases God's power. God says to Paul, in verse 9, "My strength is made perfect in weakness". In a paradoxical way, when we are at our worst God's power is much more evident. It's like a diamond's gleam which is more brilliant when set against a black velvet cloth, God's power is more evident when set against the dark backdrop of suffering. I've been preaching for 26 years now, preparing sermons week in and week out. And I can recall times when I had nothing. The reservoir was empty. And Sunday was around the corner, and the pain of that emptiness drove me to my knees in desperation, and I can recall that many times in the blackness of despair I preached with an unusual liberty of the Spirit and an unusual sense of impact on the congregation. I understand Paul's words, "I will take pleasure in my infirmities that the power of Christ may rest upon me." (v.9) The suffering of Good Friday was the backdrop for the greatest demonstration of God's power in history --- the Resurrection on Easter Sunday. There is likely no greater testimony of the power of God to a watching world than a follower of Jesus Christ responding to pain and suffering with a spirit of grace and patience.

The Temporal Nature Of Suffering

Verse 10 says, "Therefore I take pleasure in infirmities, in reproaches, in needs, in persecutions, in distresses, for Christ's sake." That's remarkable. "I take pleasure...". There's something much bigger than pain. It's Christ and heaven and eternity. Paul suffered much for the cause of Christ. He experienced beatings, stoning, imprisonment, shipwreck, and the death of loved ones. Yet in 2 Corinthians 4:17 he makes a remarkable statement. He calls his suffering, "our light and momentary afflictions". Suffering is temporal. He goes on to say "they are achieving for us an eternal glory that far outweighs them all". Romans 8:18 carries the same thought : "I consider that our present sufferings are not worth comparing with the glory that will be revealed in us". How can Paul say that?

Imagine that on January 1, of this year, you had an unimaginably terrible day. Suppose you got robbed. You got a root canal. Your basement flooded. You totalled the car. You got a reassessment from the tax man that you didn't pay enough tax. Your stock portfolio dropped by 50% in one day. And that's just the first day of the year. It's like the title of that kids' book, *"Alexander and the terrible, horrible, no good, very bad day"*. What a horrible start to the year. But imagine, from January 2 up until today, and every day from now till the end of the year, you get nothing but terrific news. Everything goes your way. Your friend wins big at the lottery and gives you half, and your struggle is whether to accept because he won it on the lottery. You get promotions and raises at work. You end up on the cover of Time Magazine and Family Magazine as Man of the Year and Family of the Year. Your wife tells you she's pregnant, and she thinks you're a super-husband. Your husband makes you breakfast in bed. Your boss gives you a three-month vacation because you're such a good employee. You get to the end of this incredible year and someone asks you how your year went. And you say, "Unbelievable." And they say, "But didn't your year start out really bleak?" And you say, "O, that was just a light and momentary setback." A lifetime of suffering in light of eternity is a light and momentary affliction.

One young man fell down a flight of stairs when he was just a baby. He lived a life of pain, and was asked, "Do you think God is fair, when you have spent so much time in pain?" The guy replied, "God has all eternity to make it up to me." One man said this, "In light of heaven, the worst suffering on earth, a life full of the most atrocious tortures on the planet, will be seen to be no more serious than one night in an inconvenient hotel." 1 Corinthians 2:9 says, "No eye has seen, no ear has heard, no mind has conceived what God has prepared for those who love Him." Heaven is the ultimate answer to the pain and suffering in the world.

God doesn't answer the question of suffering with a philosophical explanation. He answers it with the incarnation of Jesus Christ. The Word --- Jesus --- became flesh and, in the words of Eugine Peterson, "moved into the neighbourhood". And he suffered every pain you or I have ever known. He was broken, despised, rejected; He felt abandoned by the Father, betrayed by a close friend; a Man of Sorrows. Isaiah says, "They hid their faces from Him"(53:3). Corrie Ten Boom wrote, "No matter how deep our darkness, He is deeper still." When you suffer you have two choices. You can turn from God and embrace your misery, or you can turn to God and find yourself embraced by the One who became sin for you.

Jesus, in the Garden of Gethsemane, is the greatest example of the appropriate way to respond to suffering. He said to the Father, "If it is possible let this cup pass from Me" (Matthew 26:39). In other words, it's natural and normal to want to by-pass suffering. In His humanness, Jesus asked that. However, His life was driven by something bigger than a desire to side-step suffering. He said, "Not My will, but Thine be done." Jesus was more concerned about fulfilling the will of the Father than avoiding the horror of suffering and the cross. The mark of maturity in our lives is when we seek the will of the Father in the midst of our suffering, rather than in seeking to be delivered from the suffering.

Veronica and Jim were a couple who served as missionaries in the country of Peru, about 625 miles northeast of Lima. Ronnie, as she was called by her friends, was 35 years of age, and at the age of 12 she came to faith in Christ. At the age of 13, she began to talk about giving her life in service as a missionary. Her dream came true, but Ronnie's major life disappointment was that she could not have children of her own. But God in His kindness, in 1994, allowed Ronnie and Jim to adopt a little boy that they named Cory. And then God doubled their blessing by allowing them to adopt a second child. A little girl this time. Her name was Charity. Just after Easter they flew to the border near Brazil to obtain the paperwork to get Charity's permanent visa. Mission accomplished, they headed back in the small Cessna plane, to the little village where they served as missionaries.

About forty minutes out from landing, something happened that would forever change the destiny of their family. The Peruvian military mistakenly decided that this small plane was carrying illegal drugs. Without any radio communication from the Peruvian Air Force, the fighter jets opened fire. More than fifty bullets penetrated the plane, and it began a downward spiral and crashed in the Amazon River. As the plane was sinking into the murky waters, Jim had enough presence of mind to pull his wife Ronnie and his little girl Charity from the sinking wreckage. It did not take him long to figure out that neither one of them was alive. A single bullet had gone through Ronnie's back, and through her heart, and that same bullet had lodged itself in Charity's skull. They were both killed instantly.

Here's a seven-month-old innocent baby and a 35-year-old

woman who had sacrificed much to go to a difficult part of the world to serve God. If you allow yourself very long to linger over stories like this one it takes you to a place of asking some hard and uncomfortable questions. Shortly before being killed, Ronnie wrote the following words in her journal: "Life doesn't always give you a storybook ending. You don't always end up with the answers to your prayer that you desire. God often chooses to do something different with your life than you envisioned. But it's ok. He's still God and He still loves you. As long as your confidence in God remains strong in the midst of all the questions and the myriad of emotions you'll be ok. He is the only one who remains constant. And life is good if you stay in His arms, God's loving arms. You may not understand where He leads but you will be safe and secure with Him anywhere. Even in death."

Study questions

1. How has this chapter helped you in your understanding of suffering?

2. Which of the four purposes for suffering did you find most meaningful?

3. Discuss the following statement: "Jesus was more concerned about fulfilling the will of the Father than He was in avoiding the horror of suffering and the cross. The mark of maturity in our lives is when we seek the will of the Father in the midst of our suffering rather than in seeking to remove the suffering."

4. How do you respond to the origins of suffering?

CHAPTER 10

DEATH:

HOW TO GET TO HEAVEN

There are two ways to get to heaven. The first is God's plan, and the second, the Moral plan, or man's plan. We could call God's plan the DONE-plan. Everything that needed to be done to assure you a place in heaven was done by Jesus Christ through His death and resurrection 2,000 years ago. The Moral plan could be called the DO-plan. Everything that needs to be done to get you to heaven --- doing good works, living a good life --- is left for you to do. The catch is that the DO-plan requires your 100% perfection from birth to death. The DONE-Plan required Jesus' perfection.

Every religion in the world fits one of these two camps. Only one faith in the world is in the DONE category. That's Christianity. Every other faith --- Islam, Hinduism, Buddhism, Jehovah's Witness, Mormons ---teaches that your welfare in the after-life is conditional on your morality in this life.

The moral plan is not a new plan. It's been around a long time. In fact, there's a story of a young, wealthy and influential guy --- a G.Q. kind of guy --- in the Bible who is a classic example of someone who was trying to ensure a heavenly future by working the Moral plan.

The Meaning of the Moral Plan

Matthew 19:16-22 tells the story. It starts, "Now behold one came and said to Him, 'Good teacher, what good thing (notice the interest in morality) shall I DO (there's the moral plan – the DO-plan) that I may have eternal life?'" (v.16) The first thing to notice about the moral plan is that it means attempting to get to heaven by doing good things --- living a good life --- and, in the example of our friend here, getting advice from good teachers. He is a classic moralist. The moral plan is one of Satan's greatest con jobs. It's a con because it sounds so right. Do good - who would argue with that?

The Goal of the Moral Plan

The aspirations of those who live according to the moral plan, are noble. This young man's goal is to have eternal life. "What must I do," he asks, "that I may have eternal life?" He wants to get to heaven. There's nothing wrong with his goal, but everything is wrong with his plan for getting to heaven. So many good people live the moral plan with noble aspirations. They want heaven. But their plan is flawed. Our friend in the story is to be especially commended, because he has some characteristics that might have suppressed that desire for heaven. First, he was rich. Verse 22 says he was wealthy. Money has a way of inoculating a person against thinking about the ultimate reality of death and eternity. Second, he was young. Verses 20 and 22 both mention that he was a young man. Youthfulness has a way of suppressing eternal issues, and producing feelings of immortality. Third, he was powerful. Luke 18:18 tells the same story, and supplies the additional biographical detail that he was a ruler. He had power and authority. He wielded control over the destiny of peoples' lives. Power has a way of going to one's head, and backburnering issues of eternal consequence. Though he was rich, young and powerful, he was smart enough to understand that life is a vapour. It is so short.

And he cared about ultimate realities.

The Standard For The Moral Plan

Jesus punches at this young man's obsession with being good. In verse 17, Jesus said to him, "Why do you call me good? No one is good but One. That is God." And Jesus takes this term "good" that is so subjective, and defines it. So long as goodness is left in the abstract we can attribute goodness to anybody. We can all come off smelling like roses, morally speaking, depending with whom we compare ourselves. But Jesus applies a concrete standard to the concept of good. He provides a measurable definition. A standard by which all goodness can be measured. He says, "No one is good, but God." There's the benchmark of goodness. It's the Holy Perfection of God. See, if you're planning to work the moral plan to get to heaven, then you need to know the absolute standard of goodness. You need to know how good you have to be. It is theoretically possible to get to heaven on the moral plan, so long as you meet the standard. And the standard is the holy, righteous, absolute perfection of God. In verse 17, Jesus says it this way, "If you want to enter into life (on the moral plan), keep the commandments." And He means keep them perfectly. That means, not only from now on, but from the moment of birth till the moment of death. One slip, one blunder, one word of anger, would mean instant disqualification. James says, "For whoever shall keep the whole Law, and yet stumble in one point, he is guilty of all" (James 2:10). So access to heaven on the moral plan is a theoretical possibility, but a practical absurdity. Our problem is not how bad we are, but how good we're not. Unfortunately, our friend in the story doesn't get it yet. He still thinks the moral plan is a good bet.

The Deception Of The Moral Plan

In response to Jesus' statement to keep the commandments, the young man blurts, "Which ones?" He doesn't get it that Jesus is describing a perfect, humanly unachievable standard, and yet he thinks it's a manageable assignment. He thinks there's a set of commandments that he can obey to such a degree that he can satisfy the perfectly holy standard of God, and qualify him for heaven. So Jesus works with him, and lobs a few sample commandments his way. "Don't murder. Don't commit adultery. Don't steal. Don't lie. Honour your parents. Love your neighbour as yourself" (v.18-19). And as Jesus talks, our friend is adding up his score, and he's feeling pretty pleased with himself. In verse 20 he says, "All these I have kept since my youth."

This young man needs to be educated, and Jesus is about to enlighten him, and it's not going to be pretty. The young man's problem is that he thinks external conformity to a set of rules is sufficient to access heaven and satisfy God. But God is not interested in external conformity to a set of commandments --- that's religion. He wants your heart --- that's relationship. In

Matthew chapter 5, Jesus said that it's not enough to not murder people. If you're angry with someone, you've broken the spirit of that commandment, because God wants your heart. Jesus went on to say that it's not enough to not commit adultery. If you look at a woman with lustful thoughts in your heart, you've broken the spirit of that commandment, because God wants your heart.

See, Jesus could have gone after the spirit of each of those commandments that he mentioned to this young man. He could have said, "You mean, you've never become angry at someone, ever? Never gotten bitter? Never had a wayward sexual thought about a woman? Never massaged the truth? Never taken something not rightfully yours, ever?" He could have asked those heart probing questions and exposed the imperfection of this young man's heart. See, man looks at the outward appearance of a person, but God looks at the heart. We measure with a yard stick, God measures with a dipstick. He goes inside, to the heart. Jesus could have exposed the nakedness of this damaged heart right there, but he didn't. He decided to expose his heart in another way. In a masterful way actually. He does it by exposing an entirely different heart issue in this young man's life. Different from all the issues about the moral plan. he has raised up to this point. Before we get to that, let's pick up another insight.

The Result of the Moral Plan

In verse 20, the young man says, "All these I have kept... What do I still lack?" This young man is still deluded. He still thinks his moral plan is watertight, and capable of getting him to heaven. He still hasn't caught what Jesus is saying. He still feels that he is a good person. Good enough for heaven. "All these I have kept since my youth." Yet, in spite of what he says, in spite of his wealth, his youthfulness, and his power, he knows something is still missing. "What do I still lack?" Sure as he is about the moral plan, he's not sure he's bound for heaven. He's restless. No matter how good he thinks he is, he still has this nagging fear that he's not ready to die. And he says to Jesus, "What am I still lacking?" He doesn't get this feeling just because of what Jesus has been saying. That feeling is evident in his opening question to Jesus: "What good thing shall I do that I may have eternal life?" Implication? "I'm missing something, and I don't know what it is." A lot of people who hope to achieve heaven on the moral plan experience that same restlessness. That same nagging fear that they're not ready to die. When I ask someone who is working the moral plan if they know for sure that they are going to heaven, they almost always reply, "I hope so, and I'd like to. But I can't say for sure." In other words, no matter how good they are, they're not sure that they're good enough. That's the problem with shooting for a standard when you don't know what the standard is. You never know if, or when, you've hit it.

It's like a salesman being told that he will be fired if he doesn't meet the sales quota, and then isn't told what the quota is. God wants you to be certain that you are heaven bound. The Bible says in 1 John 5:13, "I write these things .... so that you may know that you have eternal life."

The Fatal Flaw in The Moral Plan

In verse 21, Jesus says to this young man, who is so determined to live out the moral plan, "If you want to be perfect...". That's a bombshell. The pursuit of perfection is the essence of the moral plan. Jesus is really saying, "Very well then, if you want to be perfect...". Jesus is describing the logical conclusion of the moral plan. If you plan to access heaven on the moral plan, then you'd better plan on being perfect. That's the fatal flaw of the moral plan. It's a plan with an unachievable goal. And because this poor guy hasn't realized this yet, Jesus exposes one clear example of the corruption in this man's heart that is so close to home for him, that he will have no alternative but to admit that he is not the model of moral virtue he pretends to be. Jesus can see inside his heart and knows that his dominant flaw is a greedy heart. So, to expose the greed, in verse 21, Jesus says, "Go, sell what you have and give it to the poor...". Jesus wasn't saying that access to heaven was contingent on giving away all your money. He's not even teaching that access is contingent on being generous, or on meeting the needs of the poor, important to God as all those things are. Because if that's what He meant then Jesus was sanctioning and validating the moral plan. But He's been doing the opposite all through this story. Besides, there are many examples of wealthy people in Scripture who loved God, and were never told to give away their wealth.

A careful reading of the text makes things clear. Jesus says in verse 21, "You will have treasure in heaven". That's a marvellous promise of eternal life that Jesus extended to this young man. And right before that He says, "Give your stuff to the poor". But here's the rub. The promise of treasure in heaven is not conditional on what He said prior to the promise, but rather on what he said after the promise. And what He said after the promise of heaven was, "Come, follow Me". Here's the full text: "If you want to be perfect, go, sell what you have and give it to the poor, and you will have treasure in heaven; and come, follow Me" (v.21). The promise of heaven is dependent on the invitation to follow Christ, not the action of giving away your wealth. More about that in a moment.

Jesus is simply illustrating that no matter how good you are, you'll never be good enough to earn heaven. And the tragedy of the story is that "when the young man heard that saying, he went away sorrowful" (v22). The problem is not that he was sad. The tragedy is that he went away. Away from the only One who could end his quest for the life he so desperately wanted, but unfortunately wanted on his terms, not God's. The fatal flaw of the moral plan is that every heart is corrupt. Romans 3:12 says, "there is none who does good". Let me illustrate this for you. We have a group of seniors at our church who carpet bowl. One day, while I was trying to pick up a few tips, one of our seniors, Bob Shaw, explained to me that every bowling ball has a bias. It's weighted on one side, and when you throw the bowl, the weight makes it turn to the right or the left. That's called the bias. The ball can't help itself. It turns because of the bias. The Bible says inside every human heart is a bias, that turns us away from God and His plan. Isaiah 53:6 says, "All we like sheep have gone astray, each of us has turned to his own way." Romans 3:12 says, "They have all turned aside". We're all biased to turn away from God just like our friend in the story. That's the fatal flaw in the moral plan. People try to work the moral plan with a biased heart, and it's not possible.

The Alternate To The Moral Plan

So much for the moral plan, and its inadequacy to access heaven. What's the solution? If not the moral plan, then what? In verse 21, Jesus says, "Come, follow Me." Jesus is saying to this young man, "I'm the alternative to the merciless, impossible, moral treadmill you're on." In John 14:6, Jesus said the same thing in different words: "I am the Way, the Truth and the Life. No one comes to the Father except through me." Jesus Christ is God in the flesh. He is the God-Man. He was virgin-born. He lived a perfect, righteous sinless life. He died on a cross to pay the penalty for your blunders, mistakes and wrong choices --- the Bible calls them sin. He offers you complete forgiveness. There is no failure in your past that lies beyond the boundary of His willingness to forgive. He rose victorious from the grave. He is alive today and, through His Spirit, lives in the hearts of men, women and children all over the world. He is King of Kings and Lord of Lords. He is worthy of your worship and the surrender of your life to Him. And He invites you also "Come, follow Me." This guy's problem wasn't that he was rich, or that he wasn't willing to give away his money. His problem was that he refused to abandon his moral plan, and he turned his back on Christ. It's not sin that keeps people out of heaven, it's a rejection of the Person of Jesus Christ. He went away sorrowful because Jesus told him to lose the money. But the real tragedy is that he lost his life. Jesus said, "What will it profit a man if he gains the whole world and loses his soul?" (Mark 8:36) Unfortunately, our friend was heartbroken for the wrong reason. He missed the point. And unfortunately that's the mistake everyone makes who is on the moral plan. They miss the whole point. The whole point of Easter, Christ and the Cross, is that you can't get to heaven without Christ.

Perhaps you're wondering where good works fit into God's plan. Does God not care about good works? Yes, He does. When you become a follower of Jesus Christ, He begins to transform your life. Goodness and good works will be part of that transformation. You will produce good works in your life, as an expression of gratitude because God has promised you heaven, not as a currency to earn heaven.

One last thing. God loved that young man. You know how much God loves you? Jesus Christ came to earth as a baby, and died on a cross, and rose from the dead, because of His great love for anyone who is religiously labouring at the moral grindstone. Dear reader, you too face a choice. Will you stay on the moral treadmill, or will you follow Christ? Jesus said, "My yoke is easy, and my burden is light" (Matthew 11:30). Jesus' way is not a moral treadmill. His way is easy and light. The Bible says, "Believe on the Lord Jesus Christ and you will be saved" (Acts 16:31).

To believe in Jesus Christ is more than a simple intellectual assent. People say they believe things all the time, but they don't really believe. For example, when someone says, "I believe we should care about the environment" but then proceeds to toss their garbage on the sidewalk, it is evident that they say they believe, but they don't really believe. There is often a world of difference between someone who says they believe something, and one who really believes. Real belief always determines behaviour. Belief in the Lord Jesus Christ means you acknowledge his Lordship and surrender your will and heart to Him as Lord and Saviour. Belief in Jesus Christ will determine your behaviour in every area of your life. You can become a follower of Jesus Christ today by expressing your faith in Him. Should you decide to make the decision to follow Christ, I have written up the following prayer as an example and to help you make that commitment to God. If these words are the expression of your heart, just pray them to God right where you are.

"Dear Lord Jesus Christ,

I believe You are God who became Man. I believe You are perfectly Holy. I believe You died on a cross to pay the penalty for my sins. I believe You rose from the dead. I believe You are alive today. I believe You are King of Kings and Lord of Lords. I believe You are worthy of my worship, my allegiance, and my surrender. I am sorry for turning away from You in my sinfulness and I humbly ask for, and receive, Your forgiveness. Thank You for the promise of heaven.

I freely surrender my heart and my will to Your command. I desire to follow Christ for the rest of my life.

In the Name of the Lord Jesus Christ I pray. Amen.

Study questions

1. How prevalent do you think the moral plan is? Why do you think so many people believe in it?

2. How often do you think about heaven? Do you think it's possible to know for sure you are going there?

3. To you, who is Jesus Christ?

4. Why do you think the moral plan is (a) bankrupt, or (b) a good plan?

5. What do you think of the following statement: "Belief in the Lord Jesus Christ means you acknowledge His Lordship and surrender your will and heart to Him as Lord and Saviour. Belief in Jesus Christ will determine your behaviour in every area of your life."

CHAPTER 11

DEPRESSION:

HOW TO GET OUT OF A BOG

Bogs suck. Literally. Bogs are ubiquitous soft patches of wet, rotting vegetation found throughout the United Kingdom, especially Ireland. Step in a bog and it'll suck you in. Depression is like a bog. Step in a patch of depression and it'll suck you in. Mind you, not all bog patches are alike, and neither is depression. Small bog patches can show up in the middle of a country path. Step in it and all you'll lose is your shoe. Some depression patches are like small bogs. They descend out of the blue, are temporal, cause only minor inconvenience, last a mere few hours, and don't interrupt the ability to function. Other bog patches are deeper, more treacherous. Step in one of these bogs, and you can be up to your waist in seconds. It can take a long time, and a lot of effort, to claw back to firm ground and escape the suction of a bog like that. So it is with some patches of depression. A person can sink fast, and surface slowly. This kind of depression can suck a person in for days at a time. It will interrupt plans, and progress. It affects function. While a person in this bog can still perform some functions, fulfilling others becomes impossible. Then, there is the Irish Bog. This is the mother of all bogs. This is the one that when you step in, it swallows you up to the neck. If it's big enough it can swallow all of you. This bog renders you powerless and unable to do much of anything to help yourself. It takes a long time to get out. Severe depression is like that. It paralyses. Normal routines end. Sleep becomes a welcome and regular diversion, and death becomes a desire. But, even these depressions deep as they are, for many people, also eventually pass.

When you get stuck in a bog --- any bog --- you need to reach solid ground. You either step or crawl to solid ground on your own, or a friend who is already on solid ground throws you a lifeline and pulls you to the safety of solid ground. So it is with depression. You need to find solid ground, or you need a friend who's on solid ground to throw you a lifeline.

There is a story told in the Bible of a man who found himself stuck in a depressive bog. His name was Elijah. His story is a marvellous encouragement to anyone who suffers from depression, and provides a pathway to solid ground.   I admire Elijah. James calls him "a man with a nature like ours" (James 5:17). He was cut from the same bolt of cloth as the rest of us. But I admire him for more than that. He's a man's man. He's the John Wayne or Sylvester Stallone of the Old Testament. He's the kind of guy that you want in your corner when the chips are down. He's the kind of guy that you ask God to send your way when your back is against the wall and all hope is lost. He's a man with a backbone, a spine of steel. He speaks truth to power, and isn't afraid to speak freely. He isn't a "yes" man. He shows up for the first time in the Old Testament, in 1 Kings 17:1. He barges onto the scene unannounced, without introduction, right into the presence of royalty. There's no preamble, no blather, no nonsense.   He declares to King Ahab, "As the Lord God of Israel lives, before whom I stand, there shall not be dew nor rain these years, except at my word."

That pronouncement sure got the King's attention, and put Elijah on his radar screen. I love that. Everything you need to know about Elijah is right there in that verse. "As the Lord God of Israel lives...". That's an unwavering belief that God is alive and well on Planet Earth. "Before whom I stand...". That's Elijah's solid conviction that God's eye is on him, and that God's power is with him. He is convinced that God is personal, that he is in God's presence, and that God cares about him, knows him, loves him and uses him.   "There shall not be dew nor rain these years except at my word...". That's a bold and confident declaration. How did he know that?   God had warned the nation back in Deuteronomy that if they rebelled, judgment would come in the form of drought on the land. The nation rebelled, Elijah claimed the judgment, and God affirmed it. So Elijah steps up in the presence of the king and speaks truth to power. No fear, no intimidation. Just boldness. A straight-up man's man.

But remember, Elijah is a man with a nature like ours. He's human. And in 1 Kings 19:1, "Ahab told Jezebel all that Elijah had done, also how he had executed all the prophets with the sword. Then Jezebel sent a messenger to Elijah saying, 'So let the gods do to me and more also if I do not make your life as the life of one of them by tomorrow about this time.'" The wife of the king puts out a contract on Elijah's life, with a 24-hour deadline. He's #1 on the queen's assassination list. This too, fits the drama of this Old Testament John Wayne. Dangerous men laugh at danger. After all we've seen of Elijah, we should imagine that this latest drama ought to be a walk in the park for Elijah. After a bold declaration with the King, the top spot on the queen's assassination list ought to be just another day at the office.

But Elijah does the strangest thing. This man's man with a strong spine of steel --- a courageous, bold, man of God --- in v.3, "arose and ran for his life". Verse 4 says, "He sat down under a broom tree and prayed that he might die." Well, who would have guessed an ending like that? Elijah is depressed. Suicidal, no less. He says, "It is enough. Now Lord, take my life." He's had enough and just wants to die. Just goes to show, anybody can get depressed. Even John Wayne. The characteristics of depression embedded in the 3,500-year-old story of Elijah are remarkable because they so accurately parallel the condition of depression in our day.

The characteristics of depression

Elijah's depression is a puzzle. It's out of character, and grips him, apparently out of the blue. He got word that Jezebel wanted him dead and he arose and ran for his life. While most people would run for their lives if the King's wife put them at the top of an assassination hit list, for Elijah, it's a massive over-reaction. There's something here that doesn't make a lot of sense. If you'd been by his side, you'd have been wondering what just happened. No explanation. No reason. He just runs. And that's the way depression is. It produces massive over-reaction. Elijah ran. Some people over-react with emotional outbursts of anger, sadness, guilt or severe withdrawal, all inappropriate overreactions to a stimulus. Depression often has no clearly defined, acceptable and understandable cause. The trigger is not necessarily the cause. Depressed people often have difficulty explaining why they feel the way they do, and may even be embarrassed to suggest an event that triggered the depression, because the event seems too petty.

I remember one day seeing a poster hanging on a wall displaying a family of ducks swimming across a pond. It was one of those double perspective pictures that showed what was going on both above the waterline and also below the waterline. The picture showed a dramatic contrast between the tranquil image on the surface of the water, and the frantic movement of the ducks' webbed feet underneath the water. The caption underneath said, "Sometimes beneath the tranquil surface lies a lot of turmoil." So it is with depression. I heard of a man just recently who went to work as usual, chatted with his co-workers, picked up some morphine tablets from the cupboard, got in his car, and subsequently threw himself in front of a train. No one had any warning, no clues, completely out of character. But such is the nature of depression.

Depression is driven by fear

Elijah ran for his life. He's scared. And he runs. And he's depressed and he wants to die. Depression is always driven by fear. Where depression is, so is fear. Fear is the first negative emotion mentioned in the Bible. In Genesis chapter three, after Adam and Eve rebelled, God asked Adam, "Where are you?" And Adam said, "I was afraid and I hid." That's what Elijah is trying to do here. He's hiding in fear. Over 300 times in the Bible God says, "Fear not". He doesn't say with any regularity, "Be anxious not", or "Be guilty not", or "Be angry not" --- only "Fear not".

The Apostle John says, "Perfect love casts out all fear" (1 John 4:18). You would expect the polar opposite of love to be hate, but it's fear. Fear prevents us from loving, forgiving and trusting people. Fear is what drives every other negative emotion. Fear is the undercurrent driving anger, anxiety, guilt, sadness and depression. Depression flows from fear. Fear of loss, aloneness, the future, or perhaps rejection.

Depression causes you to withdraw from people

Verse 3 says, "he left his servant there, but he himself went a day's journey into the wilderness". He walked for a full day. That's a long walk. By himself. That's a classic description of depression. Withdrawal. Aloneness. That's not to say all aloneness is a sign of depression. Jesus said, "Come away with me to a quiet place, and rest" (Mark 6:31). In other words, if you don't come away, you'll come apart. Jesus spent forty days in the wilderness being tempted by the devil. Withdrawal is not intrinsically harmful. The reason for withdrawal will determine whether aloneness is redemptive or debilitating. Depression compels you to be alone, because the energy loss that accompanies depression produces an inability to engage and interact with people. A depressed person will leave a phone unanswered, ignore a ringing doorbell, and neglect invitations to social gatherings.

The other emotions that flow from fear --- anger, jealousy, anxiety, guilt, etc. --- fuel the withdrawal. This creates huge relational problems. Friends and family members take the withdrawal personally, interpret the withdrawal as rejection, and may consider the depressed person rude and anti-social.

A further complication to this withdrawal symptom is when a depressed person has a high need for relationship. Some people are pre-disposed to be highly independent, and have little need for relational interaction. These people can function for long periods of time alone, and are content to do so. When this type of person gets depressed, the withdrawal is not apparent since it is not really distinct from their normal behaviour. However, when a highly relational person becomes depressed, not only do they create massive misunderstandings, there is a deep longing for those relationships in the heart of the depressed person, yet there is an inability to reach out. This is one of the paradoxes of depression, and produces profound loneliness.

Depression breeds hopelessness and despair

Verse 4 says "he prayed that he might die, and said, 'It is enough! Now Lord take my life...'". Here is the classic description of depression. Fantasizing about dying. Thinking about dying.

Wanting to end it all. Thinking "I've had enough". That's what he says. "It is enough." "I can't take any more." "I can't hang on any more." This is the belief that life is not worth living. This is the point at which every suicidal person arrives. A complete bankruptcy of hope. An utter feeling of despair. A belief that things will never change, and will never get better, and will always be like this. The thinking goes like this: "Even if I keep hanging on by my fingertips, I'm always going to feel this way, and so what's the point?" Elijah's words, in v 4, when he said, "I am no better than my fathers", may imply that his forefathers suffered from the same despair and hopelessness.

Depression breeds hopelessness, and hopelessness is a loss of perspective. Because what a depressed person believes just isn't true. The miracle of life is bigger and more valuable than any pain, no matter how great the pain. There is hope. There is always hope. There is always a light in the darkness. There is always help. There is always a way out and a way through. But the sure way to never find it is to end it. God said, through the Psalmist, speaking of Moses and the Israelites standing at the Red Sea, pinned down with the mountains on either side and the Egyptian army behind, "Your way was in the sea, Your path in the great waters, and Your footsteps were not known" (Psalm 77:19). God had a way through, when everyone else thought it was hopeless.

Depression produces feelings of uselessness and worthlessness

Elijah says, "I am no better...". Most of us like the feeling of usefulness. We all like to be able to help. Depression produces a feeling that you have nothing of value to contribute. This contributes to the withdrawal symptom. If you feel that you have nothing worthwhile to contribute to another person, in word, deed or expression, then there is no motivation to connect.

Depression causes a loss of energy and appetite and change in sleep patterns

The only time you don't feel the weight of depression is when you sleep. And so you sleep much. More than you need. More than is helpful. Sleep was designed by God to restore energy, and recharge batteries. But too much sleep drains the batteries, like leaving the rechargeable batteries on the charger too long. Elijah went to sleep. Verse 5 says, "As he lay and slept under a broom tree...". He likely lay under the tree to get shade, which means he's sleeping in the middle of the day. Depression slows down the brainwaves, and produces a loss of energy and constant tiredness. Suddenly an angel touched him and said to him, "Arise and eat." Apparently he hasn't eaten in a while. And with excessive sleep often comes a loss of appetite. And God provided food for him to eat. But after he ate, he went back to sleep again.

Depression can make you feel like you're lugging an extra 150 pounds of baggage around with you. Consequentially, what you would be able to accomplish ordinarily with no problem, now requires enormous effort when you are in a depressed state. Doing a load of laundry feels like you're bench-pressing beyond your limit. Ironically, while depression provides much insight and material for writing a book on depression, the depression can threaten to prevent the book from actually being written. Depression makes writing feel like you're running against the wind in a wind tunnel, with the turbos on full blast, or punching underwater, or arm wrestling The Hulk.

Depression produces disappointment

Or maybe disappointment produces depression. It all gets mangled up together after a while. Elijah says in v.10, after God asked him, "What are you doing here, Elijah?", "I have been very zealous for the Lord God of Hosts, for the children of Israel have forsaken your covenant, torn down your altars, and killed your prophets with the sword. I alone am left, and they seek to take my life." And then if you jump down to v.13, you see that God asks him the same question, "What are you doing here, Elijah?" And Elijah answers with exactly the same speech : "I have been very zealous for the Lord God of Hosts, for the children of Israel have forsaken your covenant, torn down your altars, and killed your prophets with the sword. I alone am left, and they seek to take my life." Verbatim. Word for word. It's like he's been rehearsing this speech in his head. We do that, don't we? If we're going to complain, or tell somebody off, we rehearse the speech in our head, and go over all the complaints and things that disappoint us, and we could recite that speech word for word, because we've practiced it so much.   He's depressed because he's disappointed, or he's disappointed because he's depressed. It doesn't really matter. Disappointment and depression are like jam and toast. Let's break down his speech for a moment. He sounds like a depressed pastor. First, he's saying he has done his best. He's worked hard.   He's been very zealous. Second, people haven't responded the way he expected. They've rejected his message, and they've forsaken God's covenant, torn down His altars.   Third, the people are making life miserable. They killed the prophets.   Not only are they not getting with the program, they're trying to sabotage the program. I heard of a pastor recently who was describing the church he had pastored, and said, "I spent the most miserable 20 years of my life pastoring that church." That's where Elijah is. And fourth, they're making it personal. "They seek to take my life." "They're praying for my funeral."   Many a pastor experiences disappointment and depression for exactly the same reasons.

Finding solid ground in the bog of depression

I ran out of emotional gas a few years ago, and during that journey rediscovered Elijah's depression. I looked carefully at how God moved him through that depression, and followed the same path as I moved across the river bed, and gradually came out the other side. Through that journey I reviewed some lessons I had learned many years earlier, I remembered some truths I had forgotten, and I learned some things I had not realized before both about myself and about the Lord and His wonderful Word.

My journey through depression patterned on Elijah's journey, and allowed me to recharge and find solid ground again. As I look back now on those days, I realize I am not the same man I was then. The Lord used depression to advance me to a new place, a better place, a place of greater freedom and position to do greater good.   I have learned/am learning to not fear depression, nor to run from it, but to face it, and stare it down, and to see how God uses it for good in my life. I can say now, "Thank you, Lord, for allowing depression to be in my life."

Now let's turn to Elijah again, and discover the redemptive journey through which Elijah moves as he experiences the value of depression. When Moses stood at the burning bush, God told him to throw down the stick which he had in his hand. When he did so, it turned into a snake. And poor old Moses ran for his life. Moses evidently hated snakes. God said, "Pick it up again by the tail." You can imagine Moses slowly turning to face this reptile that he profoundly fears, and reaching down to grab it by the tail. That would take even more courage, because the last place you want to grab a snake is by the tail. And yet, because he was willing to face his fear rather than flee his fear, God honoured him and turned the snake back into a stick. And what a stick that would become. That was the staff that Moses stretched across, and was used by God, to split the Red Sea. It was the same staff that he held up over the battlefield when the Israelites fought the Amalakites and gave the Israelites victory. It was the same staff with which he hit the rock and water flowed out. And this was the staff he was running from. That which you fear the most is often the source of God's greatest blessing. Your depression may well be the source of God's greatest blessing in your life, if you'll move toward it and face it, and stare it down, and not fear it. Depression is not a sign of weakness. It's an opportunity to display God's presence and power.

Step 1- Identity-Know that God loves and cares about you

The bog of depression convinces a person that he is alone. That no one understands, or cares. That no one really knows him. That no one can help, or even if they could, nobody wants to help. The first thing God does for Elijah is to reassure him that Someone is there, and does care. There is One who is great and good, and is in your corner, and is able to accomplish whatever concerns you. The first thing God does for Elijah is to convince him of God's attention, tender love and care. Notice v.5, "As he lay and slept under a broom tree, suddenly an angel touched him." And in v.7, "the angel of the Lord came back a second time and touched him." That's a beautiful word. "He touched him." That's the touch of attention, concern, care, and love. Jesus displayed this same expression of love and concern in His ministry. Everywhere He went He touched people.

Even a man's man needs to know he's loved, and that his life matters to somebody. That somebody cares. People don't care how much you know, until they know how much you care. Even successful people at the top of their profession long to know that somebody cares, and is willing to reach out with a meaningful touch. The first thing God establishes for Elijah is the matter of his identity. And the first step in moving toward solid ground in the bog of depression is to cement your identity. Satan uses depression to attempt to torpedo your identity with sinister lies such as, "You're useless, and worthless. Nobody knows you, loves you or cares about you. You're finished. Your future is bleak, and holds the prospect of impending doom." Yet the Bible is filled with truths that clearly establishes your identity. Jesus said, "You will know the truth and the truth will set you free" (John 8:32). Here are some statements regarding the truth about your identity taken from Psalm 139 : God knows you. He is with you. He made you. He has an intentional plan and a purpose for your life. He loves you. He understands you. He forgives you.

The best way to make these truths a part of the fabric of your thinking and life is to embed them in your mind through Scripture memorization. As an assignment, try memorizing Psalm 139, a few verses a week.

Step 2 - Physical wellness - Eat, drink and exercise

God is really practical. A car doesn't work without fuel, and neither does your body. It needs food, water and exercise to survive. Depression attacks the appetite and exercise, so in verse 5 the angel asks Elijah to "arise and eat", and "....so he arose and ate and drank, and he went in the strength of that food...". It's no accident that the angel causes Elijah to focus on food and water first. Food, water and exercise are the fuel of good health. In Daniel 1:12,15, Daniel says "Please test your servants for ten days, and let them give us vegetables to eat and water to drink.....And at the end of ten days their features appeared better and fatter in flesh than all the young men who ate the portion of the king's delicacies."

Since your body consists of 70% water, eight glasses of water a day is required to keep all the systems in your body operating at optimal levels. Trying to deal with depression while neglecting food and water is like trying to diagnose the problem in a car engine with no oil in the motor and no gas in the tank.

Exercise matters. If exercise seems like a daunting task, start small with an attainable amount. Walk around the park, or the block. If that's too much, then walk around the house. Elijah was too drained to start the journey the first time the angel came to him and he went back to sleep. He had to try again. If at first you can't do it, try again the next day.

Step 3 - Define Reality - Come to your senses

The Word of the Lord came to Elijah, and He said, "What are you doing here, Elijah?" and a second time God asks in   v. 13, "What are you doing here, Elijah?" Notice that God calls Elijah by name. The sound of your name triggers a powerful emotional response. It's a lot different from saying, "Hey you, Buddy", or "Sir", or "Ma'am", or "Miss". Saying your first name is even more powerful than saying your last name. When your teacher calls out your last name, you're no different from any other student in the class. But when the teacher has you by yourself, and calls you by your first name, there's a different emotional response. When she quietly says, "John, is everything alright?", that resonates. You think, "She knows me. She cares about me." When God calls Elijah by name, He is affirming the same thing the angel confirmed when he touched Elijah. Then He says, "What are you doing here?" Now, God isn't asking that question because He doesn't know the answer. God knows exactly what Elijah is doing there. God knows he's depressed and wants to die. He's asking the question because He wants Elijah to formulate the question for himself. He wants Elijah to look in the mirror and ask himself, "What *am* I doing here?"

God asked Adam a similar question in Genesis 3, when He said, "Where are you?" (v.9). God knew where Adam was. He was asking Adam if Adam knew where Adam was. That's what everyone who is on a journey of self-destruction must ask. "Where am I and how did I get here?" God wants Elijah to ask the same question. He needs to look with clarity at his situation and ask, "How did I get myself into this mess?" He needs to define reality.

There's a marvellous description of this principle in the story of the Prodigal Son. After the younger son leaves home with his father's money, he runs to a far country, blows all he has, finds a job as a pig handler, and becomes so starved that he wants to eat the pig food. He has no friends, no money and no self-respect, and is on the verge of starvation. The first step in the journey back home and a redemptive outcome occurs in Luke 15:17, when "he came to his senses". He said to himself, "What am I doing here?" He defined reality. He looked in the mirror and said "How did I get myself into this mess?"

Every journey back towards health and wholeness includes this step. This is the first step every alcoholic takes when they work the 12-step program of Alcoholics Anonymous (AA). He stands up in front of a small group and admits, "My name is _____ and I am an alcoholic." They define reality. This is the first step people drowning in alcohol, debt or any other addictive behaviour must take if they are to regain control of their lives. They must face the fear and clearly define reality. A person with mounting financial debt has to face the demons of credit card statements and overdue bills and add them up and discover with clarity how much is owed. This is a challenging step for many people. Some simply deny that a problem exists. Others diminish the problem, downplay its seriousness, and pretend it's under control. Others disguise the problem. They know there's a problem but they won't admit it to anyone else and they mask it, so that no one else will know. Others deflect the problem. They blame the cause of the problem on other people, thereby absolving themselves of any responsibility for solving the problem, and in doing so, relinquish control of their own destiny.

One definition of insanity is to do the same thing the same way over and over and expect different results. The second step in the AA 12-step recovery process says that choosing to keep going on the road you are on is insanity. That's what you call defining reality. Unfortunately, pain is often the only motivation that gets our attention sufficiently to create real change. Kevin Miller in his book *Hunger for Healing*, said that he wasn't prepared to admit that he needed to change until "the acid of my pain ate through the walls of my denial".

I had a friend who wore a comfortable old pair of shoes so long that the sole began to come apart at the toes. He refused to wear any other shoes, since he had become so fond of those old shoes, worn out as they were. He and I were headed into a store one day when the entire sole of his shoe ripped open. He had to walk around that store that day, lifting his foot like a duck, with the sole flapping up and down like a cow's tongue. He finally said, "I guess it's about time I got a new pair of shoes." Sometimes we will not change until the pain of staying the same becomes greater than the pain of change.

Depressed people are often reluctant to admit that they are depressed, even to themselves, probably in large part due to the social stigma of depression. There seems to be almost a paranoia about depression. Depression is perceived as a sign of weakness. The only thing we need to fear about depression is the fear itself. This refusal to clearly define depression stands as a massive blockade to redemptively handling depression and finding the way back to solid ground. You cannot resolve a problem until you clearly define the problem. A problem clearly defined is a problem half solved.

Here is a suggested prayer to help you process this step.

"Dear Heavenly Father, I am depressed. I am sorry for not facing up to this before now. Perhaps I lacked courage, or was afraid. Perhaps I never realized before now that I was depressed. But I admit it today. I am not running from my depression any longer. I am not going to deny it, diminish it, disguise it, or deflect it. I am not going to be intimidated by it. I want to face it with courage and faith. My depression has caused me to make bad decisions that have produced some unfortunate consequences. For these, I am sorry. I was wrong. Please forgive me. Thank you for allowing depression to be part of my life. I trust by faith that You can use this depression to fulfill Your purposes in my life. Give me the courage and wisdom that I need to respond appropriately to my depression. Amen."

Step 4-Surrender-Adjust your expectations and demands

In the narrative of Elijah's depression, verse 11 tells us that God told Elijah to go out and stand on the mountain, and then "....a great and strong wind tore into the mountains.... and after the wind an earthquake.... and after the earthquake a fire followed by a fire". But the text says God wasn't in the wind, the earthquake or the fire. That's a surprise. If God is about to show up, we would expect Him to show up wrapped in one of those cataclysmic events, or in some other sensational fashion. Undoubtedly, Elijah would have been expecting God to show up in one of those great cataclysmic natural phenomena, in a powerful display of His Greatness. We are like that. We expect God to evidence His presence in great cataclysmic ways. We say, "God, if you're really there, get me out of this mess." Or some such thing. What a disappointment to discover that God wasn't in the earthquake, the fire or the wind ! Unmet expectations, and their kissing cousin, unrealistic demands, are common causes of depression. God said, "My thoughts are not your thoughts, neither are your ways My ways" (Isaiah 55:8). Paul said, "How unsearchable are His ways beyond finding out?" (Romans 11:33). It is almost a certainty that our expectations will be different from God's desire for us.

Aspirations that I had in my heart 20 years ago are far different from the reality of what I experience today. We need to release our list of expectations of what we think will cure our problems and our unhappiness, and give it to Him. Abraham had something that was more precious to him than life, and God tested him to see if it mattered more to him than God. In Genesis 22, God said, "Take your son, your only son, the son whom you love and sacrifice him to me" (v.2). God wanted to see if Abraham would trust Him, and the only way to do that was to ask if he was willing to give up his most precious possession. Heb 11:19 tells us that Abraham trusted God so much that he figured if he did as God said, God was big enough and good enough that He could resurrect his boy and give him back.

Surrender your expectations and release your demands. What is it that you think will make you happy? What are your expectations? What are you waiting for God to do? Are you disappointed in God? Will you lay all your expectations and demands on the altar?

Read over the following prayer, and if it is the expression of your heart then pray it in your spirit.

"Heavenly Father, I surrender all of my expectations and demands and lay them at Your feet today. I confess that I have been disappointed in You and other people because of some unfulfilled expectations. I have been angry because my demands have not been met. I am sorry, I was wrong, please forgive me. You are not my slave, I am Yours. I want from this day forth to do Your bidding, not to have You do mine. I want Your will for my life, Your purposes. Not my will but Yours be done. Amen."

Step 5-Abide-Discovering God's Presence in the Stillness

In verse 12, the record says, "after the fire, a still small voice....". Well, who could have seen that one coming? Who would have expected it? God shows up in a still small voice. Elijah discovered God in the last place he expected --- a still, small voice. That was God's Presence. Isn't it interesting that in the bog of depression Elijah encounters the presence of God with the whisper of a still small voice? Remember Moses' staff? That which we fear the most is sometimes the source of God's greatest blessing. Depression can be your friend, and a source of great blessing. God can speak to you in the stillness of your depression.

A butterfly was trapped between two panes of a sliding glass window. He battered his head against the two pieces of glass for what seemed like an eternity, trapped and unable to get out. He finally grew tired of flying, and slowly began to drop lower and lower in the window frame. When he reached the lowest point at the bottom of the window, he discovered that the outside window was opened a crack. He quickly went through it and flew to freedom. He would never have found the way to freedom if he hadn't been brought very low. So it is with depression. Sometimes we make the most valuable discoveries only when we have been brought very low.

Step 6 – Contribute - Do something good

We were made to do productive work. God put Adam in the Garden of Eden, and told him to work it and take care of it. When we do meaningful work, it makes us feel good. Conversely, when we stop doing meaningful work, it contributes to our depression. In verse 15, God gives Elijah a redemptive assignment. It's an opportunity to make a meaningful contribution. God says to Elijah, "anoint Hazael as king over Syria... anoint Jehu as king over Israel...". God is telling Elijah, "I have a job for you." God has a plan and a purpose for Elijah. We all need to feel useful. This is an important step in the process of moving through depression.

Ephesians 2:10 says, "We are God's workmanship, created in Christ Jesus to do good works." When God assigns you He also equips and empowers you. He told Elijah that He had "reserved 7,000 in Israel" (1 Kings 19:18). God always has resources we know nothing about. And He wants to use you. But you have to start moving.

Here are eight areas to consider, that may require a redemptive contribution from you. What can you begin to do today, that would redemptively contribute, or bring order, to each of these areas? Try designing one goal that would help bring order to any of these areas that have gotten off track. --- Your Finances. Your Recreation/hobby. Your Property. Your Job. Your Health. Your Relationships. Your Ministry.

One assignment that God has given every believer is to be an active contributor at your church. Ephesians 4 says the Body grows "as each one does its part" (v.16). Your church needs you. We all need each other. You may be wondering how you can go about getting involved at your church. Here are six things you can do, starting now, to take a hold of the rope at your church, without waiting for someone to give you a job:

1.Pray for the church daily. 2.Share your faith with a friend who doesn't go to church. 3.Help another brother or sister grow. Share what you know. 4.Love. Encourage, write a note, make a phone call. 5.Volunteer --- when the church announces a need for volunteers volunteer, or ask if there are any needs. 6. Contribute financially.

Step 7 – Community - Find a friend

We were made for community. When God created Adam, He said, "It is not good for man to be alone" (Genesis 2:18). God designed us to need each other. That's why the Church is called a family. We were made to function best in the context of relationship. A coal burns brightest when it's surrounded by other burning coals. It burns out when it's isolated and left to burn alone. We too burn brighter when in the heat of community. Verse 19 says Elijah "departed from there, and found Elisha". From that time on, Elijah and Elisha become comrades. This is one of the foundational principles of AA, and why that organization has been so helpful to so many people. That's an example of the supportive power of community.

One writer said it this way:

> "The neighbourhood bar is possibly the best counterfeit that there is to the fellowship Christ wants to give His church. It's an imitation, dispensing liquor instead of grace, escape rather than reality --- but it is a permissive, accepting, and inclusive fellowship. It is unshockable. It is democratic. You can tell people secrets, and they usually don't tell others or even want to. The bar flourishes not because most people are alcoholics, but because God has put into the human heart the desire to know and be known, to love and be loved, and so many seek a counterfeit at the price of a few beers. With all my heart," this writer concludes, "I believe that Christ wants His church to be unshockable, a fellowship where people can come in and say, 'I'm sunk, I'm beat, I've had it.' Alcoholics Anonymous has this quality --- our churches too often miss it."

God designed the Church to be a safe, supportive community that provides spiritual heat and encouragement, and stimulates greater health. I would encourage you to make finding a friend, or community, to support and encourage you a front-burner priority.

Step 8 – Discipline - Develop an hour of power

Wise choices are always character-driven, not emotionally driven. The goals of emotionally driven decisions are either the avoidance of pain or the pursuit of pleasure, or both. The goals of character-driven decisions are more noble. The Book of Proverbs says, "A man who has no discipline is like a city without wall" (25:28). A city without walls is a city without protection, honour or self-respect. So it is with a person who has lost the ability to make character-driven decisions.

So how do you get started on the journey of making character-driven decisions? The answer is one hour at a time. Develop an hour of power in the course of your day. Spend one hour a day moving through a series of character-driven decisions, resulting in a series of wise and healthy activities. Here is a suggested list to get you started.

1. 5 minutes to review the identity truths from Step One

2. 5 minutes of Prayer

3. 5 minutes of Bible study

4. 5 minutes of worship and praise

5. 5 minutes of Scripture memorization

6. 5 minutes of exercise

7. 5 minutes to improve something

8. 5 minutes to phone a friend

9. 5 minutes to schedule a daily healthy eating and drinking plan

10. 5 minutes to serve the Church

11. 5 minutes of recreation

12. 5 minutes of reading something healthy

Study Questions

1. How would you describe depression?

2. What did you learn about depression from this chapter?

3. Which of the characteristics of depression seem most familiar to you?

4. Why do you think Elijah got so low that he wanted to die?

5. How encouraging is it for you to realize that Elijah experienced such realistic symptoms of depression?

6. Respond to the following statement: "Depression breeds hopelessness, and hopelessness is a loss of perspective. Because what a depressed person believes just isn't true. The miracle of life is bigger and more valuable than any pain, no matter how great the pain. There is hope."

7. Which of the steps to recovery did you find most helpful and why?

8. Which step do you think would be most challenging to fulfill?

9. How does God's dealing with Elijah help you in your relationship with God?

CHAPTER 12

FINISHING WELL

In Barcelona in 1992, on the evening of August 3, Derek Redmond broke fast from the starting blocks in lane five, and made up the stagger on the runners in lanes six through eight. Then Redmond's hamstring popped in his right leg. As the other runners finished the race, he lay motionless on the track. The world watched as Redmond's father, who had been in the grandstand, came across the track and helped his son to his feet and walked with him across the finish line. That moment would become known as one of the most glorious finishes in Olympic history. Failure doesn't have to prevent a fine finish.

Finishing well is a glorious thing to watch. Finishing badly is unfortunate, if not tragic. I think of people who started out with such promise, such potential, such lofty dreams, such high hopes and grand ambitions, and somewhere along the way they got themselves lost. They lost their bearings, lost their moral moorings, lost their passion, lost their faith, lost joy, lost hope, and seem to be finishing so poorly --- spiritually, relationally, financially, marriage-wise and business-wise. It's easy to start well. It's another thing entirely to finish well.

In this chapter, I want to talk about finishing well, not in the short term, but ultimately. Have you considered what it means to finish well after decades of running this race we call life? In 2 Timothy 4, the Apostle Paul gets at the business of finishing well when he says, "I am already being poured out like a drink offering and the time of my departure is at hand" (v.6). The drink offering was the last of a series of ceremonial offerings in the Old Testament sacrificial system. Paul was simply saying, "My life has been a series of sacrifices, and now I'm on the last one." And then he gives us a picture of what finishing well looks like.

Finishing Well Means Having No Regrets

Paul says, "I have fought the good fight" (v.7a). What a thing to say at the end of the race. A loose translation of Paul's words might run something along these lines: "I fought well. I did my best. I rolled up my sleeves and got involved in the battle. I didn't sit on the sidelines, and complain about all the things that were wrong, I made a difference." Remember Theodore Roosevelt had a similar sentiment when he wrote, "Far better it is to dare mighty things, to win glorious triumphs even though chequered by failure than to rank with those poor spirits who neither enjoy nor suffer much because they live in the gray twilight that knows neither victory nor defeat."

One of the most tragic situations in life is coming to the twilight years, riddled with regrets about all the things we wish we'd done, but never got around to. The unwritten book, the unsung song, the unsaid apology, the unpracticed instrument, the untaken course, the unmade phone call, the unspoken encouragement, the unbooked trip, the unexperienced parachute jump, the unbroken habit, the unpracticed habit, the unenjoyed prayer life, the unopened Bible, the uncelebrated worship.

When Paul asserts that he fought the good fight, it infers that he took care of all the priorities in his life that mattered, and that he did his best to do all that God had called him to do. No regrets.

Second, he maintained a steady, prevailing spiritual pace with no unfinished business

Paul goes on to say, "I have finished the race" (v.7b). Sometimes when you say "I'm finished" that's not a good thing, because it means you are giving up. But there are other times when I say "I'm finished" and that is a good thing. When I'm working on a project and I've accomplished what I set out to do, and cleaned everything up, I stand back and say, "I'm finished". That means there's no unfinished business left to be taken care of. That's what Paul has in mind here. There's no unfinished business. I have finished the race.

Third, he maintained a prevailing, life-transforming faith

Paul makes a marvellous declaration of the purity of his faith as he reaches the end. He says, "I have kept the faith" (v.7c). The faith in Jesus Christ that was birthed on the Damascus Road and brought joy and love and peace and purpose and meaning and life change into his life was still growing when he got to the twilight of his life. I love to hear a man say that about his wife, after 50 years together, "I'm more in love with her today than ever". And what a thrill to hear a person say, "I've been walking with Christ for 50 years, and I'm more in love with Him than ever."

I don't suppose there is any greater way to finish than to cross the finish line and hear the Lord Jesus Christ say, "Well done, my good and faithful servant."

Fourth, he had an unwavering assurance of heaven

Paul is absolutely convinced that heaven is in his future. He says, "there is laid up for me the crown of righteousness…" (v.8). There is no fear for Paul, of what lay on the other side of the doorway of death. I sat by the bed of an old saint some years ago, as he lay near death's door. He said, "I've been waiting my whole life for this moment. This is why He saved me --- to prepare me for this moment." That's finishing well.

I love to sail. Years ago, I would occasionally spend the night on the lake, in the dark, damp, cold mist. By morning I was glad to motor back towards the marina where I would come into the dock, and I longed for that moment when I would step ashore. I came across a poem some years ago that gets at the same idea. It goes like this.

"O think to step ashore

And find it heaven

To clasp the hand outstretched

And find it God's Hand

To breathe new air

And that celestial air

To feel refreshed

And find it immortality

Ah! to think to step from storm and stress

To one unbroken calm

To awake and find it home."

That's finishing well.

Fifth, he was surrounded by a few trusted friends

Paul, at the end of his life, had one of the most precious gifts imaginable --- the gift of a few loyal friends. He writes, "Be diligent to come to me quickly... Only Luke is with me. Get Mark and bring him with you..." (v.9-12). Solomon, writing in Ecclesiastes, says, "Two are better than one... if one falls down, his friend can help him up" (4:9-10). Finishing well is being surrounded by a few close friends.

I remember a funeral being conducted at our church many years ago, and only two sisters and a brother were in attendance at the funeral, besides the minister. It rained that day, and the three debated for many minutes whether to bother going to the cemetery, before finally succumbing to guilt, and admitting, "We never spoke to him while he was alive. The least we can do is stand in the rain for him." What a tragedy to get to the end of life with no friends. Make friends while you have time. And remember, the best way to make friends is to be a friend.

Sixth, he was still Involved in ministry

Paul is thinking about strategic ministry right up to the end. He writes, "he is useful to me for ministry" (v.11b). He has no thought of retiring from ministry. He's still looking for ways to serve. Paul reminds me of the little lady, eighty years of age, doing missionary work in the Caribbean, riding a motorcycle over the mountains. I know a wonderful man, 80 years of age, in admirable health, who has cleaned stuffed drains, and removed

P-traps in the toilets at our church, because that's part of his ministry. We have a group of seniors at our church who pray every Wednesday night for all the prayer concerns in the church family. They are finishing well.

Seventh, he was still growing

I love this characteristic of Paul, as he draws to the close of his life. He instructs Timothy to, "Bring the... books, especially the parchments" (v.13). If Paul were writing in our day, he might say, "Bring me the DVDs, the CDs and the videos. Bring me those magazines on leadership, and marriage, and character, and money, and raising kids." Howard Hendricks tells the story of an elderly lady friend who when she meets Hendricks, says, "Howie, tell me about the best five books you've read in the last year." Make a point of reading stimulating books, and keep growing.

Eighth, he had no bitterness

One of the greatest poisons to the human spirit is bitterness and disappointment. Paul knows nothing of unforgiveness when he writes, "....all forsook me. May it not be charged against them" (v16). Everybody deserted him. He could have blamed and shamed. But he refuses to finish poorly ; instead, he follows the lead of his Lord and Master, who said, "Father, forgive them." He may also be remembering the example of Stephen, whom he watched being stoned to death, who said, "Lord, do not charge them with this sin" (Acts 7:60). So many people grow bitter, instead of better. They hold grudges, and complain. Finishing well is to have a gracious, forgiving spirit.

Ninth, he was still devoted to Christ

The secret to Paul's ability to not become bitter lies right here in the little comment, "the Lord stood with me and strengthened me" (v.17-18). Right to the end the relationship that mattered to Paul more than anything was his love relationship with Christ. And this love relationship with Him was the fountainhead for his ability to love people. This business of loving Christ is the hallmark of finishing well. I hear people say, "I wonder what people will say about me when I die." A question of far greater importance is "What will Jesus Christ say about you when you die?"

So what's the secret? How do you finish well? The secret lies in what you do every day from now until you die. What you do every day, from this day on, is determining more than anything else how you will finish. In a marathon, the way you pace yourself every mile of those twenty-six miles has profound bearing on your capacity to finish well. Finishing well in a marathon is determined not by any spectacular accomplishment at any particular juncture along those 26 miles of rugged terrain. Finishing well in a marathon is determined, among other things, by setting a wise pace and plodding along at that wise pace, mile in and mile out. Finishing well in the marathon of life is not primarily determined by the accomplishment of a few spectacular feats, here and there. Rather, it is determined primarily by the sorts of activities you engage in, day in and day out, for the few thousand miles you have available to run this race. Perhaps you've gotten a little tired along the way, a little disappointed perhaps. Maybe you started out with a burst of enthusiasm, but things have become stale. There's nothing really wrong. It's just that there's not much joy, or service or contribution, or commitment. Would you look over the qualities of finishing well and say, "Lord, what do I need to do every day, that will ensure that I finish well?"

Perhaps you've been living badly --- not wickedly or cruelly or immorally --- just badly. Perhaps because of wrong choices and poor management you're on a course that is certain to finish poorly if something doesn't change. Maybe you're a little like a sailboat in a race that has been blown off course. You need to recalibrate and make a mid-course correction. Should you stay on that course you will not finish well. Maybe you think it's too late. You think you've been blown off course for too long to finish well. You need to know there is nothing that has occurred in your past that makes it impossible for you to finish well. You see, the Bible says we were all on a course that was going to finish badly, very badly. Isaiah 53:6 says, "All we like sheep have gone astray" because of sin. Romans 6:23 says, "The wages of sin is death". But Romans 5:8 says, "While we were still sinners Christ died for us". He died so that you wouldn't have to die. He didn't come to remind you of your mistakes and rub them in; He came to rub them out. He didn't come to finish you off; He came to give you a chance to finish well. Jesus Christ wants to hear you say, "Lord Jesus Christ, I believe in You, and I surrender my life to You. I am sorry for my sin. Please forgive me."

Five years ago I was thinking about this matter of finishing well, and I scrawled some thoughts down on paper. Here's what I wrote:

"I want to finish well. I want to finish with a vibrant growing marriage. I want to grow into a deeper love relationship with my wife, and be a source of strength, hope and encouragement to her. I want to be a dad who modelled the love of Christ to his kids, and enabled them to become men and women of strength and integrity. I want to raise kids who will never doubt the love of their father and mother, and who will take their place in this world, free from the need of people's approval, but intent only on the Heavenly Father's approval. I want to finish with true friendships, with whom I can practice authentic love and honesty. I want to finish with a growing relationship with Christ ---developing in love and faith and always increasing the Fruit of the Spirit in my life. I want to be free from the bondage of living under the burden of other people's expectations and for other people's approval. I want to live for an Audience of One. I want to finish with the full understanding that I am loved and accepted by the only One who really matters, and who said, 'I will never leave you nor forsake you'. I want to love people with absolutely no expectation of anything in return, beginning with my wife, and my kids. I want to finish with healthy disciplines. To steadily establish new habits that will prevail, and that will steer my life in a direction that will maximize the potential God has wired into me.

I want to craft sermons that will feed my congregation. I want to let the sermon percolate through me, before it crosses my lips. I want to keep growing as a pastor. I want to learn new skills to make me a better preacher and shepherd.

I want to be free of emotional baggage and insecurities. I want to be authentic. I want to be transparent in the pulpit and in private. I want to be able to say, 'Here I am, warts and all.' I want to be able to share hurts and struggles in a redemptive way that will help others. Most of all? I just want to finish well. I don't want to have to say, 'I wish I'd spent more time with the kids.' I want to be able to look into my wife's eyes at the finish line and say; 'I was never unfaithful to you. I loved you as hard as a man knows how.' I want to be able to look my kids in the eye and say, 'I did my best.' I want to be able to look into the eyes of my congregation and say, ' I loved every one of you, and I treated you with dignity and honour and fairness.' I want to be able to look into the eyes of Christ, and hear Him say, 'Well done, my good and faithful servant.'"

That's my prayer for you too, dear reader, that you may finish well.

Study Questions

1. If you were to write a "Finishing well" list what would it look like?

2. What do you think of the statement: "It's easy to start well. It's another thing entirely to finish well"?

3. What have you always wanted to do, but have never done yet? What would it take to make it happen?

CHAPTER 13

TORTOISES AND FENCE POSTS:

MY STORY

I am a Belfast boy, born and raised on the outskirts of Belfast. The people responsible for naming the areas where I grew up were colour fascinated. I lived in an area near Green Island, which was near Greymount. Greys Lane led to my area called the Whitewell, where I lived in a neighborhood called the White City, with streets filled with white houses, but none with white picket fences. The nearest beach was called Whitehead, which was a ways from Black Rock. But, of course, Ireland is most famous for its beautiful green landscapes, and is known as the land with the 40 shades of green. Perhaps you've heard of the tourist who visited Rome and found a telephone in the middle of the street on a golden column with a sign over it announcing, "Direct line to Heaven: $1000 per call." He went all over Europe and found the same golden telephone, with the same sign, "Direct line to heaven: 1000 Euros per call." He got to Belfast, and found the same golden phone, and the sign said, "Direct line to Heaven: 25 pence." He asked one of the locals, "How come, all over Europe, this phone is 1000 Euros for a call to Heaven, and here it's 25 pence?" The man answered, "Son, you're in Ireland now. It's a local call." The Bible describes heaven as a garden environment, and I've often wondered if it has Ireland's 40 shades of green.

Unfortunately, Belfast wasn't a heavenly city after 1969, when "The Troubles" started. For years, Belfast was known around the world for bombs, bullets, thrown bricks and burning buses. As a wee boy my best friend was John MacFarland. He was Catholic. I was Protestant. I didn't know what those labels meant. I just knew that's what we were. I used to walk up the Serpentine Road every Friday night with him after school. The two of us would pull his wee cart full of empty bottles to the Catholic Church on the Antrim Road, and get them filled with holy water. I always thought that was the Catholic equivalent to the petrol station. My dad took the car to the petrol station, and I assumed the Catholics went to the holy water station. The big Catholic Church was intimidating with its incense and bells. I naturally assumed that the Catholic Church was all about bells and smells. I didn't know what the difference was between Catholics and Protestants, except that I knew they were different.

Shortly after the troubles started, John and I were around 10 years old, and we were told we weren't allowed to play together anymore. That's when I first discovered how different we were. I discovered then, that Ireland was a place of conflict and prejudice, all because of ancient claims to real estate between Britain and the South of Ireland, over the North of Ireland, and that it went back over 300 years to King Billy and the Battle of the Boyne. I remember thinking, "What's the good of religion? If religion is all about fighting, and prejudice and hatred, rather than the way to connect with God, then religion is useless."

At 17, I started an apprenticeship at Harland and Wolff Shipyard. That's where the Titanic was built. I worked for eight months at Gate Nine, where the blocks and tackle were stored that were used on the cranes that built the Titanic. At least, that's the story that went around anyway. I can remember that first paycheck from Harland and Wolff: 30 pounds a week. I bought my first car a few months later - a Mini Minor. The reason I bought that car was because I was fed up riding the Double Decker bus downtown to the Queen's Quay and into the heart of the shipyard every morning, in the dull, grey, Irish drizzle, wearing my navy blue overalls --- my boiler suit. We called them boiler suits, I think, because you got so hot you boiled in them. That Double Decker bus was crammed full every morning, downstairs and upstairs, with shipyard workers in navy blue boiler suits, and lunchboxes underarm. Some lunchboxes were the size of Volkswagons. I remember one morning scoring a rare seat on the bus beside a shipyard old-timer. He said to me, "How long you been working at the shipyard, son?" and I said, "Just started a couple of weeks ago." Then I asked, "What about you?" He said, "Fifty years now. Been riding this bus down the Queen's Quay for fifty years. Just a couple more months and I'm done." I couldn't get those words out of my head. I can still hear him saying that, "Been riding this bus down the Queen's Quay for fifty years." I remember thinking, "Surely there's more to life than this." I'm not suggesting there's anything wrong with working at the same company for fifty years. In today's economy, that would be a blessing and a miracle. It was just that it seemed to me that there had to be more to life than just a job, and riding the same bus for fifty years.

I emigrated to Canada, along with my mother and father, in May, 1979. I was eighteen, and didn't take long to find my first job, as an apprentice tool and die maker. My first paycheck was $200. The equivilent to about 100 pounds. I graduated from making 30 pounds a week to 100 pounds a week, inside of two weeks. I thought Canada was the Promised Land, and the greatest country in the world. I still do. And it is. We are so blessed to live in this great country, in spite of the politicians. And in spite of the rising levels of immorality and godlessness in every level of the culture, we are privileged to call ourselves Canadian.

About a year after coming to Canada, my dad developed medical problems and returned to Ireland with my mom. That left me in Toronto at nineteen, pretty much to my own devices. I was at crossroads, and could have gone in a number of directions. That raised another question for me. What in the world am I doing here? What's the point of life? As I stood at the crossroads, someone kindly put a book in my hand called *The Late Great Planet Earth* by Hal Lindsey. This friend simply said it was a good book and that I should read it. There's an important lesson right there. Never miss an opportunity to do a kind deed, when the Spirit prompts you. You never know how God might use it. When you're prompted to give someone a helpful tract, book or resource, just do it. You never know the context of the person's life into which you drop a good deed. Lindsey's book was just what I needed. That's where I discovered that the Bible contains dramatic prophecies that are being fulfilled in our day. The Bible prophesied that Israel would become a nation again.

That happened in 1948. The Bible says that the Jewish people will return to their homeland. That's been happening for the last 60 years. The Bible says that Israel will be at the epicentre of the last great war of Armageddon, where Israel's neighbours will come against her in one great Military Alliance. I could see, even thirty years ago, that Israel was the epicenter of the Middle East, as it is today. I remember Lindsey saying in his book, "The Bible is more up to date than tomorrow's newspaper."

Lindsey's book began to answer another question for me. What makes the Bible different from any other book? Why can the Bible be trusted? Aside from the stunning fulfillment of prophecy, that's when I discovered that the Bible is actually not one book, but rather 66 books. They were written by over 40 different authors, over a 1,600-year period, in three different languages, on three different continents. And the amazing thing is that in spite of that diversity of authors, languages, geography, and time, the storyline of the Bible is about one central Person --- the hero of the Book --- Jesus Christ of Nazareth. That would be like taking a class of 66 students, putting them in 66 separate classrooms, and assigning each of them the task of writing one chapter of a book to create a total of 66 chapters. But you don't tell them anything about the storyline of the book. You don't provide them with any information regarding setting, genre, or characters in the book. And you prohibit anyone from collaborating with any other student in the class. Then, when the chapters have been written, collected and assembled into a "book" of 66 chapters, imagine if each of those chapters when merged together, told one cohesive, sensible story, with a solid consistency of character and theme. In fact, if those student assignments did contain a common theme and consistency in character, we would naturally assume that someone had to provide collaboration between each of the writers. It couldn't happen any other way. That is exactly the claim the Bible makes for itself. God provided collaboration with 40 authors over 1,600 years to tell the redemptive story contained in the Bible, with a consistency of theme, and a central Character, named Jesus Christ. In the Book of Genesis, Jesus appears as the Seed of the woman. In Exodus, He is the Passover Lamb. In Joshua, He is the Commander of the Lord's Army. In Ruth, He is the Kinsman Redeemer. In the Psalms, He is the Good Shepherd. In Proverbs, He is Wisdom. In Matthew, He is a King.

In Mark, He is a Servant. In Luke, He is a Saviour. In John, He is God. And on and on, all through the Bible, until the Book of Revelation where He is the Alpha and the Omega, the First and the Last, the Beginning and the End, the Lion of Judah, the Lamb of God, the One who is worthy to receive worship and praise, and adoration. That's why the Bible is trustworthy. The unity of theme in the diversity of authors indicates supernatural authorship.

Then, there's The "Human Authorship" evidence that substantiates that the Bible can be trusted. Our judicial system is heavily dependent on the testimony of witnesses. And every courtroom goes to great lengths to ensure that a witness's testimony is true. The witness must first promise to tell the truth, the whole truth and nothing but the truth. Then, the witness's credibility, or believability, is established. In fact, if a witness is caught in a lie, the entire testimony is usually deemed to be worthless, because credibility is lost. Courtrooms rely on various kinds of witnesses to provide testimony. Expert witnesses offer opinions on a particular matter, such as a medical doctor giving an opinion on a medical issue. Eyewitnesses typically give firsthand accounts of something they saw, heard, or experienced. The Apostle John was an eyewitness. He opened up his first little epistle by saying, "That which was from the beginning, which we have heard, which we have seen with our eyes, which we have looked upon, and our hands have handled, concerning the Word of Life --- the life was manifested, and we have seen and bear witness, and declare to you" (1 John 1:1-2). John is giving eyewitness testimony to that which he saw, heard and experienced concerning Jesus Christ.

At 19, I wasn't sure that I believed the resurrection of Jesus. Then someone pointed out to me that the testimony about the resurrection of Jesus does not derive from one person, but rather nine people, most of whom claimed to be eyewitnesses of the resurrected Christ. Nine people wrote the New Testament where the testimony about the resurrection of Jesus is found. So to reject the facts of the resurrection is to reject the testimony of nine people. Imagine if you were sitting in a jury with eleven of your peers, listening to a criminal case, and nine eyewitnesses came to the witness box, and each witness gave essentially the same basic facts about what they saw, heard and experienced, and that those testimonies established the guilt of the accused. Furthermore, the defense offered no testimony to rebut the testimonies of the other nine witnesses. It would be hard to imagine any jury not bringing a swift conviction. So it is with the compelling resurrection testimony of the nine New Testament writers. To reject the New Testament accounts of Jesus Christ and His resurrection is to believe that these nine men fabricated the stories they wrote. It's significant also, that eight of these nine New Testament authors were executed because of their written claims about the life, death and resurrection of Jesus. The ninth, John, was imprisoned on the Isle of Patmos, a kind of 1st century Alcatraz, directly because of his testimony about Christ. Tradition tells us that the Apostle Peter, when he was about to be crucified, asked to be pinned upside down, as he was unworthy to be killed in the same manner as his Lord. His wife was supposedly crucified before his eyes, shortly before he was killed. All this because of their testimony about Christ.

All this raises the question, why would anyone willingly die for something they wrote and testified about, if they didn't believe it to be true? History demonstrates that men are prepared to die for a cause they believe to be true, but no man will willingly give their life for something they know to be a lie. The New Testament is true because these men were eyewitnesses, who died for what they wrote about Jesus Christ of Nazareth. The Old Testament is true, because Jesus put His stamp of approval on the Old Testament in the record of the New Testament. He said, "I have not come to abolish the Law and the Prophets, but to fulfill them... one jot or one tittle will by no means pass from the Law till all is fulfilled" (Matthew 5:17-18). So if Jesus is credible, the Old Testament is authentic.

I discovered also that the Bible could be trusted because it had the ring of truth. You know how when you hear something, sometimes it doesn't ring true, it just doesn't sound right. On the other hand, sometimes you hear something, and it does ring true, it sounds right, it makes sense. When I began to read the Bible and learned what it said about any topic, whether it was how to build a quality marriage, how to order your finances, how to be a good employee, how to be a better person, how to be a great leader, how to have a terrific sex life, how to deal with conflicts, how to deal wisely with your kids, how to survive in a tough world, it had the ring of truth. It made sense. And that's what you would expect if a book really is a supernatural book written by God Himself. This book is unlike any other book in the world.

That led me to the next big question : what must I do with this Book? The whole point of the Bible is to guide people to the person of Jesus Christ. Jesus said, in John 5:39, "You search the Scriptures for in them you think you have eternal life, and these are they which testify of me." A GPS is a marvellous piece of technology. It can guide you from your house to your destination, giving you precise instructions at every turn. The Bible is God's GPS --- God's Positioning System. The Bible can guide you straight to Jesus Christ and ultimately to heaven.

On a winter Sunday night in November, 1980, at Peoples Church, I met Jesus Christ. The preacher that night explained Romans 3:23, which says "All of us have sinned...". That didn't surprise me. I already knew that. I haven't met anybody who doesn't believe that. Everybody knows that nobody's perfect. But it was the second half of the verse that was news to me. "All fall short of the glory of God." God's Glory is God's holy character, and that verse says everybody falls short of that. That's the part that most people don't get. Almost everybody thinks, or hopes, they're good enough to get to heaven. But the Bible says, "All fall short...".

Imagine a long ladder leaning against a high wall. Let's say the bottom of the ladder represents evil and the devil, and the top represents Good and God. (It has always fascinated me that there is one letter difference between "devil" and "evil", and "God" and "good".) And then imagine some benchmarks along the rungs of the ladder. Let's put the most evil human beings imaginable on the bottom rung, just above Satan. Guys like Hitler, Idi Amin, bin Ladan would be down there. Then near the top, let's put the most pure human beings you can think of. One rung down from the top, people like politicians and lawyers. Just kidding. Maybe Billy Graham, or your mother. Now I'm a pastor. I get paid for being good. Everyone else is good for nothing (just a joke). Let's put me half way up the ladder. And let's put you a bit above me. Now watch this. Right at the top of this ladder is Jesus of Nazareth. He is perfectly righteous, pure, and holy. He's sinless. The Bible says the only way to get to heaven is by living a perfectly holy life, equal in perfection to that of Jesus of Nazareth. In baseball language that would mean, morally speaking, that you would be batting 1000, and no errors, ever. All the way from birth to death. This is what Romans 3:23 means when it says, "All have sinned and fall short of God's glory." Remember, the problem is not how bad we are, it's how good we're not.

And there's nothing we can do to save ourselves. Ephesians 2:1 says that we were dead in our trespasses and sins. And dead people can't do much to help themselves. I remember the first time I visited Niagara Falls. That's where I tasted Kentucky Fried Chicken and Root Beer for the first time. I remember looking across at the American side of the Falls and getting drenched by the spray coming off the updraft, and getting deafened by the roar of the Falls. The Bible says this sin has separated us from God. Isaiah 53:6 says, "All we like sheep have gone astray. Each of us has turned to his own way." It's like we are standing on the Buffalo side of Niagara Falls, and God is on the other side. (Notice I put God on the Canadian side.) And there's a great gulf between us called sin. And we can't cross this gulf by ourselves. Imagine we all decide to leap over the gulf by taking a running jump. Some will get a lot further than others. But really, at the end of the day, what difference will it make? No matter how fast we run, or how far we jump, or what distance we get, we will all fall short, and all end up plunging into the Niagara River. Romans 3:22 says, no matter how good you are, "there is no difference". And the Bible says this separation from God is the reason for every problem of the human heart. This is the reason for all loneliness , emptiness, anxiety, guilt, lack of fulfillment, lack of purpose, anger, frustration, sadness, and depression. But 2,000 years ago, Jesus came to earth and died on a cross, and He became the bridge between earth and heaven. Romans 5:8 says, "While we were still sinners, Christ died for us." He died to offer us forgiveness for our sins and bring us back into relationship with God. 1 John 1:9 says, "If we confess our sins, He is faithful and just and will forgive us our sins and purify us from all unrighteousness". There is no blunder, no mistake, no failure, no wrong choice you have ever made in your life that lies beyond the boundaries of God's willingness to forgive. No matter how far you have strayed from God, His grace reaches further. And He offers you a home in heaven forever. Jesus said, "Let not your hearts be troubled. Believe in God, believe also in Me. In My Father's house are many mansions, and I am going there to prepare a place for you." (John 14:1-2) John 3:16 says "For God so loved the world that He gave His only begotten Son, that whosoever believeth in Him should not perish but have eternal life." Our good works can't get us to heaven. Only Jesus can. Ephesians 2:8-9 say, "For it is by grace you have been saved through faith, and that not of yourselves, it is the gift of God, not by works, so that no one can boast." Jesus said, "I am the Way, the Truth and the Life. No one can come to the Father except through Me" (John 14:6).

People say all roads lead to heaven. But they don't. All roads lead to God, where He will act as Judge. There's only one road to heaven, and that's through the Person of the Lord Jesus Christ. The preacher that night at Peoples Church explained that the Bible said the Lord Jesus Christ, and His death, and His offer of forgiveness and eternal life, was a gift. Romans 6:23 says, "…the gift of God is eternal life". And a gift to become yours must be received. If I offer you a pen as a gift, that gift only becomes yours when you receive it.   Receiving and believing in Scripture mean the same thing. John 1:12 says, "But as many as received Him, to those who believed on His Name, He gave the right to become children of God." You receive Jesus Christ when you believe. Romans 10:9 says, "If you confess with your mouth the Lord Jesus, and believe in your heart that God has raised Him from the dead you will be saved."

When our kids were small, I announced one night that we would go for ice cream. "But first," I said, "you must pass a test." I took them to the bottom of the basement stairs and said, "If you can get from the bottom of the stairs to the top of the stairs we'll go for ice cream. But first some rules. You can't touch the stairs, nor the sides of the stairs, nor the handrail, nor the walls. Now, if you can get to the top of the stairs without touching any of these things I'll take you for ice cream." They looked glum for a bit until the oldest said, "I got it. Dad, bend over." And he jumped on my back and said, "Get up the stairs, donkey." And up we went. The second born said, "Dad, get back down here." And we did the same thing. Then the girls followed the pattern. When they were all at the top of the stairs, and pleased that they had passed the test, and that ice cream was on the agenda, I said, "Now, there's a lesson in all this." Our firstborn said, "I knew this had something to do with the Bible." I said, "Just as you were at the bottom of the stairs helpless to get to the top, so we are all at the bottom of the stairs, helpless to get to heaven. 2,000 years ago, Jesus came to the bottom of the stairs, and bent low and put a cross on his back, and carried it to Calvary, so that He could carry you to heaven. That's why Jesus said, 'No one can get to the Father except through Me.'"

The preacher closed the meeting that night at Peoples Church by telling a story about two men journeying through life. One was an atheist, the other a follower of Jesus Christ. He said, "The Christ-follower spent his entire life loving God, praying for his wife and kids and friends. Reading and obeying the Scriptures. Serving in his church. Trying to develop the character of Jesus in his life, by being honest, and a man of integrity, and kind, and loving. Trying to build his marriage and family on the bedrock of obedience to Holy Scripture. Telling friends that Jesus loved them." The preacher asked, "Suppose the Christ-follower dies and discovers he was wrong. There is no God, no life after death, no heaven, no hell. That all his prayers for his wife and kids and family and friends turned out to be a waste of time. All the years he spent trying to live a life worthy of the Saviour, being a man of character and helping people, was for nought. Telling his kids that they didn't ever need to be afraid of death, that there was another world out there beyond this one, and that God had set eternity in their hearts and that they were made for that world, was all futility. All the times he told friends about God's love towards them was a waste of effort. He just goes into a hole in the ground and that's it." Then the preacher said, "If he was wrong, what has he lost?" Answer? Nothing.

Then he said, "The atheist, on the other hand, went through life rejecting God, even becoming hostile towards the God he didn't believe existed, and mocking those who did have faith." The preacher went on, "Now, suppose the atheist dies, and he discovers that he was wrong. There is a God. There is a heaven and a hell. There is a judgment. And that all those times when a follower of Christ came alongside of him and gave him a tract or an invitation to a church event, it wasn't mere happenstance, but rather God's amazing grace, gently getting his attention." Then the preacher said, "If the atheist is wrong, what has he lost?" Answer? Everything. Then he quoted Jesus' words, "What will it profit a man if he gains the whole world and loses his own soul?" (Matthew 16:26) Someone once said it this way, "He is no fool who gives what he cannot keep to gain what he cannot lose."

And that night, I stood and stepped out into the aisle, and walked to the front of the church and gave my heart and my life to Jesus Christ, and I've never looked back, and He's never failed me, left me, or disappointed me. He's guided me, directed me, provided for me, loved me, helped me, and gifted me. He has blessed my life beyond measure. He has given me a beautiful wife and four great kids. I love my wife and kids more than life itself, but I love Him more. I have never regretted for a minute the decision I made to receive Christ, thirty-one years ago.

Stephen Hawking, the most brilliant physicist in the world, announced in his last book that there is no God. I've always liked Hawking, and when I read that, I thought, "Well, if Hawking says there is no God, I guess I should quit my job then, and go do something else more meaningful." 25 years' worth of preaching sermons was an exercise in futility, according to Hawking. You know why Stephen Hawking doesn't believe in God? Because he's never met Jesus Christ. If he met the Jesus he's never known, he would meet the God who is sovereign, and all powerful, who can raise the dead, and heal the blind, deaf, mute and maimed. If Jesus had kept going He would have rid all Israel of all disease. What more could Jesus have possibly done to provide empirical evidence to prove that He was the Son of God, and God in the flesh?

If Hawking met Jesus, he would see the God who fed 20,000 with a boy's lunch, who suspends the laws of physics and walks on water and calms storms. He would know that One who gives grace to moral failures, and kindness to people that society has disenfranchised, and who speaks love to wounded women and hopeless men. He would see the One who taught with a wisdom and moral authority that caused people to be astonished. He would see Jesus, the One the Book of Revelation calls The Alpha and The Omega, The First and The Last, The Beginning and The

End. The Lion of Judah, the Lamb of God. The Saviour of the World. The One who Was, and Is, and Is To Come. The One before whom one day, every knee will bow and every tongue will confess that Jesus Christ is Lord. Stephen Hawking has spent his life studying the Laws of Physics. One day he will meet the Lord of Physics, and he will bow the knee to Jesus Christ. He'll either do it voluntarily, or by necessity. The only reason I believe in God and Hawking doesn't is because I have met Jesus Christ.

I feel a bit like a tortoise on a fence post. A rural doctor tells the story about the time he was stitching up the hand of a 75-year-old Norfolk farmer, who cut it on a gate while working cattle, and the doctor struck up a conversation with the old man. Eventually the topic got around to Gordon Brown and his appointment as the British Prime Minister. "Well, you know," drawled the old farmer, "this Brown fellow is what they call a fencepost tortoise." Not being familiar with the term, the doctor asked him what a fencepost tortoise was. The old farmer said, "When you're driving along a country road and you come across a fence post with a tortoise balanced on top, that's called a fencepost tortoise." The old farmer saw a puzzled look on the doctor's face, so he continued to explain, "You know he didn't get up there by himself, he definitely doesn't belong up there, he doesn't know what to do while he is up there, and you just have to wonder what kind of idiot put him up there in the first place."

Well, that may well be true of politicians. But there's truth here for all of us. We didn't get here by ourselves. Somebody put us here. I didn't get to the place in my ministry and life by myself. God, in His marvellous grace, love and kindness put me here. We're all tortoises on fence posts. Everything we enjoy: our marriages, our kids, our jobs, our homes, our savings, our health, were given to us by God. He put us here, and He gave us all that we enjoy. We would do well to hold everything loosely, in an open, grateful hand, not in a clenched fist. The Bible says, "The Lord giveth and the Lord taketh away. Blessed be the name of the Lord" (Job 1:21). We're good with God's giving part, not so good with the taking part. But blessed be the Name of the Lord. The Lord is good, and the Lord is great. And the Lord can be trusted to know and to do what is best.

CONTACT THE AUTHOR

For more information or to obtain a list of other reurces, you can contact Roy in any of the following wys:

By phone: 416-251-6121

By email: wroy@rogers.com

Our website: www.queenswaybaptis.on